Editor-in-Chief

Rayon D. Scarlett

The Universal Slang Dictionary was collectively gathered by and from real people from all walks-of-life, (ex; inmates, correctional officers, criminals, law enforcement, cashiers, street hustlers, music artists, movie actors, etc.)

The slang words in this dictionary were examined by people from areas across urban and suburban communities in the United States. Keep in mind that slang is created every day and might reflect the region that it was created in. We are more focused on the universal slang that every urban community can relate to because the term has become so popular and frequent.

This dictionary will grow with time to include new entries from more diverse regions describing their current slang. The chief editor spent time on both types of blocks so we understand where it all came from.

We would love to hear your thoughts and feedback so please contact us by email with any comments or suggestions: theuniversalslangdictionary@yahoo.com

I0776118

Introduction

The Universal Dictionary is the first of its kind to document the latest prison and street slang used every day by everyday people. Slang words are usually documented long after everyone is fully aware of their meaning. The entries contained in this dictionary come from the edge of society where slang is developed at its fastest rate. Words and phrases have been drawn from many sources, including but not limited to:

- The streets

- Jails/prisons

- The criminal underground

- Social media trends

- Pop culture

- Hustler terms

- Derogatory terms

This dictionary is intended to break the language barrier between urban and corporate America, forging a better communication between the average American and our urban culture. Every entry in this dictionary has been researched and authenticated in-light-of the most current slang, and the way it is used today.

Explanatory Notes

The heart of this dictionary is the A-Z Jail/Street slang vocabulary section. Readers will find information about common and/or proper spelling, pronunciations, synonyms, and meanings. It is divided into two distinct sections, each of which is a distinct body of work, Jail and Street, each with its own alphabetical order.

•	The Jail Slang section contains words and phrases commonly used in jails and prisons across the United States.

•	The Street Slang section contains words and phrases drawn mostly from urban regions within the United States.

Some entries are included in both sections due to how common their use has become on both sides.

This dictionary is divided into two sections, which starts with the Jail section in the beginning. Currently, the Jail section is shorter. Wherever possible, we have attempted to format this book like other dictionaries. This was done to make it easier to use by those familiar with that layout.

Symbol Key

a	Entry Title

b	Pronunciation

c	Part of Speech

d	Alternate Spelling

e	Introduction to a Definition

f	Definition Number

g	Example Sentence

\\   Used in pairs to mark the beginning and end of a transcription

'   Marked at the beginning of the syllable with the strongest degree of emphasis or stress

.   Marked at the beginning of the syllable with the second strongest degree of emphasis or stress

·   Mark of a syllable division in pronunciation

__   Insert boldface entry word

ↄ   Indication to add a word, i.e. a possessive noun or pronoun

Ex: (a)street \ (b)'stret \ (c)n: (d)streets (e): (f)[1]referring to anywhere outside of a correctional facility or police custody: [2]local neighborhood in a city or town : [3](phrase) "in the __" ; lifestyle of alleged criminal activities : [4](phrase) "__knowledge"; common sense learned on or about the streets "see definition[2]" Ex: (g) [3]<Ron spent his teenage years in the streets.>

Many entries contain multiple definitions which are notable by superscripted numbering. Many entries will be accompanied with an example sentence, so the reader can see how the entry word is most commonly used. On the entries that have multiple definitions, a superscript number will be placed at the beginning of the example sentence which will match the superscript number of the definition that it's describing.

The spelling of a word when used as a slang may be spelled in many ways. In the Universal Slang Dictionary, the entries are spelled how it sounds or the most common way that it appears from the people that use the word. Ex: "ease dropping" is the slang spelling for "eaves dropping". We try to associate both spelling when possible to help the reader with pronunciation.

You might see slang words that mean something totally different when it is used in a phrase. Ex: "on his top" means to annoy someone, but "top" by itself means to receive oral sex.

Changing the tense of a word can also alter the meaning. Ex: "squashing ᴄᴐ beef"; a possessive noun or pronoun must replace ᴄᴐ to indicate whose beef is being squashed.

Pronunciation Symbols

Symbols	Examples	Symbols	Examples
ə	**a**bout, c**o**llect, supp**o**se	n	**n**ine, sudde**n**
'ə, ˌə	h**u**mdr**u**m	ŋ	si**ng**, i**n**k
ər	butt**er**, f**ur**ther	ō	t**oe**, holl**ow**
ă	h**a**t, p**a**tch	ŏ	s**aw**, p**o**t
ā	p**ay**, f**a**te	ȯr	b**oar**, p**or**t
ä	f**a**ther, br**o**ther	oe	French b**oeuf**
âr	c**are**	oi	n**oi**se
är	c**ar**, h**ear**t	p	**p**e**pp**er, **pop**
au̇	t**ow**, **ou**ch	r	**r**oad
b	**b**a**b**y, **bib**	s	**s**auce
ch	**ch**ain, fet**ch**	sh	mi**ss**ion, **sh**ip
d	**d**ip, a**dd**	t	hoppe**d**, **t**ie
ĕ	st**e**p, p**e**t	th	**th**in, e**th**er
ē	b**ee**, **ea**sy	th	**th**is

f	fifty, **ph**rase	ü	b**oo**t, f**ew** \fy**ü**\
g	bi**g**, **g**ate	ŭ	c**u**t
h	**h**and, a**h**ead	ůr	p**er**m, **ur**ge, f**ir**m, w**or**d, h**ear**d
hw	**wh**ich, **wh**ale	ue	French r**ue**
ĭ	p**i**t, t**i**p	v	**v**i**v**id
îr	p**ier**, h**ear**	w	a**w**ay, **w**ith
ī	b**i**te, p**ie**	y	**y**ellow
j	**j**u**dg**e	z	**z**one, **x**ylophone
k	**k**i**ck**, **c**oo**k**	zh	vi**s**ion, plea**s**ure
l	**l**i**l**y, need**l**e		
m	**m**ur**m**ur		

JAIL

SLANG

ac status \'a-c-stā-tes\ *abbr*: administrative custody, (Inmates are isolated from the rest of the jail population)

ah gun \adj: referring to a person who is good at what they do <my lawyer is _>

ah hit \vb: an inmate being denied parole\release from prison <my brother got _ because he got a write up.>

already \: ¹yes: ²you already know

Aryan Brotherhood \'a-re-en·bre-ther-hud \ n: white supremacist gang

Aryan Nation \ n: white supremacist gang

assed out \'as-ed·out \ vb: ¹being out of luck: ²to lose ²<they __ when they lost their millions>

banger \ 'ban-er \ n: a sharp knife-like object or ice pick made with contraband supplies <an inmate got stabbed with a __>

bang out \ 'ban- 'aut \ vb: to stab someone <he was about to __ his friend turned foe>

ball \ 'bȯl \ vb: to show up and do big things, or to start a game <they came to __>

bawling \ 'bȯl-in \ adj: [1]strong bad smelling odor: [2]balling [1]<after a soccer match he was __>

berd \ adj: black nerd

B.G.F. *(acronym)*: Black Guerrilla Family (gang name)

[1]bid \ 'bid \ vb: doing time in jail <doing a __ in prison>

[2]bid \ 'bid \ n: someone to pick on or being made fun of <he was the __ of the day>

bidding \ 'bid-in \ vb: [1]doing time with sense of joy: [2]enjoying life with someone Ex: playing cards [1]<they were __ all night>

birdbath \ vb: [1]washing up from a sink or basin: [2]to freshen up without taking a shower [1]<he took a __ before his visit>

Black Panthers \ n: civil rights group

blade \ 'blād \ n: [1]a homosexual: [2]joint

block \ 'bläk \ n: a housing area for inmates in jail or prison <there are dozens of __ in prison>

block card \ n: a written warning before a write up <the inmate got a __ for talking loud in the dayroom>

block hugging \ vb: not leaving the dayroom or spending most of your time on the block in prison <Rob never goes to the yard, he __>

block runner \ n: inmate worker who cleans the block <the __ cleaned the block>

blood in \ vb: shedding blood to get acceptance in a gang, usually the '*Bloods*' <before becoming a Blood, you have to __>

bloods \ 'bləds \ n: gang wearing red <He is a part of the __.>

blue devil \n: the prison phone located on the blocks *(usu. inmates get into fights or arguments over the phone with family members or other inmates and the phones are mostly blue in state prisons.)

bombing da bubble \ 'bäm-in-da-bə-bəl \ vb: the act by inmates of throwing things at the *control booth* <inmates got mad and started __>

boofing \ 'bü-fing \ vb: to hide something in the anal cavity <he was __ drugs>

booked \ 'bük-ed \ vb: [1]to get in trouble: [2]arrested or go to the hole [1]<Dave got __ for fighting.>

books \ büks \ n: inmate account <he had $50 on his __>

bootlicker \ 'büt-liker \ adj: an inmate who seeks to gain favor by flattering a C.O. <he is a __>

booty bandet \ 'bü-tē-ban-dət \ n: a homosexual that rapes others <he is a __>

bread \ 'bred \ n: money (same as the street slang, "bread") <even food is __ in prison>

bricks \ 'brikz \ n: the outside world, streets <he had two days left before he went back to the __>

brown \ 'braůn \ n: slang for tobacco <he smokes __>

bubble \ n: an isolated control room for a block

buckhorn \ n: 'bək-hȯrn \ n: [1]cigarette: [2]a roll up: [3]tobacco

bucket \ 'bə-kit \ n: [1]the hole: [2]jail or prison [1]<he went to the

buckeye \ 'bə-ˌkī \ n: [1]an inmate that caters to a C.O.: [2]the oppressor's companion [1]<he is a __>

bucking traffic \ vb: [1]to buck traffic: [2]to cut in line in front of someone: [3]cutting someone off

bullpen \ 'bu̇l-pen \ n: [1]waiting area in a court house for prisoners: [2]small holding cell for inmates [1]<they waited in the __ to see the judge>

[1]**bum** \ 'bəm \ adj: or **bummed**: [1]a poor homeless person [1]<he is a __>: [2]someone who lacks skills: [3]to borrow something [3]<he bummed a cigarette from his friend.>

bum rush \ 'bəm-rəsh \ vb: to surprise attack a person <__ him>

bunkie \ 'bənk-ie \ n: a cellie that shares a bunk bed <Jack didn't like his __>

burn \ 'bərn \ vb: [1]when an inmate's privileged activities are cancelled: [2]to get cheated out of something [1]<the C.O. __ us>

butch queen \ [1]one who acts like a girl and looks like a man: [2]drag queen

caddie \ 'ka-dē \ n: cigarette or tobacco <let me get a __>

captain \ 'kap-tən \ n: the commander of the surges and Co.'s <__of the troops>

cashin a check \ 'kash-sin-ə- 'chek \ vb: or to **cash a check**: [1]to masturbate: *(syn)* [2]cashin out: [3]jerk off [1]<his cellie was caught __ in his cell.>

cashin out \ 'kash-sin-'aů̇t \ vb: or **cash out**: [1]to masturbate: *(syn)* [2]cashin a check: [3]jerk off [1]<he's addicted to cashin out>

catch reck \ 'kach-'rek \ vb: or **catching reck**: fight, stab or shoot <Bob loves to catch reck>

cat burglary \ 'kat-'bər-glə-rē \ vb: entry into a place to steal cunningly or trickily when no one is there <he waited until everyone left to commit the __>

cat thief \ 'kat-thēf \ n: a person who sneakily, slyly, cunningly, or trickingly steals <the __ stole my food in my house>

cellie \ 'sel-lē \ n: an inmate's roommate <the two cellies got along>

Cell restriction \ vb: being restricted in his or her cell for x amount of days as a form of punishment

cell slug \ n: an inmate that stays in his cell most of the time

c.e.r.t *(acronym)*: [1]correctional emergency response team: [2]the jail version of a SWAT team

chaw \ 'chaw \ n: [1]mainline: *vb:* [2]place to eat [2]<they went to __>

check-in \ 'chek-in \ vb: [1]to go into protective custody: [2]P.C. [1]<Q __ because of his charges>

chet \ chet \ n: [1]a child molester: [2]chomo: [3]tree jumper

chi chi \ chē-chē \ n: [1]food made in a bag using ramen noodles: [2]jailhouse meal [1]<they ate a __>

chomo \ 'cho-mō \ n: [1]child molester: [2]chet: [3]tree jumper

chump \ 'chəmp \ n: gay or homosexual <he's a __>

C.O. *(abbr)*: correction officer

Cock gazer \ 'käk-'gāz-ər \ n: an inmate who looks at another's private parts: **-gazing** <he was cock gazing>

commissary \ 'kä-mə-iser-ē \ n: a store of food supplies and cosmetics for inmates <bought food off __>

contraband \ 'kän-trə-ˌband \ n: prohibited items, usually things not issued by the D.O.C. or purchased off commissary <he had __ in his cell>

control movement \ 'kən-'trōl \ vb: verbal control of inmates' movement by telling them to stand in front of their cell before they can go eat or other recreational activities or telling them to walk in a single file line

control panel \ - 'pa-nəl \ n: booth located on each block to control the cells and/or other activities

Cora check \ 'kōra-'chek \ vb: a bravery check to see if a person has heart; heart check

cosmetic \ 'käz-'me-tik \ n: skin care and hygiene products <uses __>

count time \ 'kaůnt-tim \ vb: the time when inmate locations are verified for security

cracker \ 'kr-kər \ n: [1]racist white man: [2]poor white man: [3]used as a derogatory term <mad __>

dance floor

.

dancefloor \ 'dans-'flȯr \ n: referring to the visiting room in a prison or jail <he went to the __ for a visit>

Date snatcher \ 'dāt-'sna-ch-r \ adj: an inmate that gets another inmate in trouble to delay his release

dayroom \ n: [1]lounge area outside the cell: [2]block

D.C. status \ *abbr*: disciplinary custody

dice \ 'dīc \ n: a target

dime \ 'dīm \ adj: 10-year sentence <he did a __ upstate>

dirt ball \ 'dərt-'bȯl \ n: an unclean person <the nasty __>

dirt box \ n: referring to the anus or butt hole <pooped out his __>

discharge \ 'dis-chärj \ vb: a term used when releasing an inmate from jail or prison

D.O.C. *(acronym)*: Department of Corrections

Doubling back \ 'də-bəl-iŋ-'bak \ vb: obtaining more than one meal tray during any one meal service period <__ at meal time>

drama \ 'drä-mə \ n: [1]referring to a violent crime: [2]a felony <my friend is in jail for some __>

drive bye \ 'drīv-bī \ vb: referring to an inmate not getting mail for the day by the C.O. that is passing it out <Ray was upset about the __>

dropping a load \ 'dräp-in-ä-lōd \ vb: [1]to take a dump: [2]to take a smash: drop a load <Rob was __ in the cell>

dub \ 'dəb \ adj: [1]20-year sentence in jail or prison: [2]the number 20
[1]<he did a ___ in upstate>

duece \ dü-s \ n: synthetic marijuana

ear hustling

.

<u>**eye hustling**</u>   **E**

ear hustling \ vb: to listen to a person's conversation secretly

eighty-eight *(acronym)* hail hitler, phrase used by white
supremacists, (88)

elbow \ 'el-ˌbō \ n: [1]life sentence: [2]L

eleven and half to 23's \ n: county shoe, skippies

eye hustling \ 'i-'hə-səl-in \ vb: [1]to watch someone doing something
secretly: [2]wanting something that someone else has [1]<___from behind
the curtains>

fem queen \ ʻfem-ˈkwēn \ n: [1]a man with woman features: [2]transgender [1]<in prison transgenders are called __>

fishing \ ʻfish-in \ vb: [1]passing items during a lock down using a line: [2]looking to start an argument or fight with someone: [3]a homosexual looking for a mate [1]<the inmate was __ a book to his friend> [2]<__ for trouble>

Five on the door \ adv: five minutes to go in and out of a cell before it's time to close it <Co.'s use __ to control inmate movement in the dayroom>

flickz \ ʻflikz \ n: pictures <showed his friend his __>

freak \ ʻfrēk \ adj: an awkward person

fuck wagons\ adj: a group of unruly inmates

<The inmates were so loud in the day room, the C.O. thought to himself, "What a bunch of _.">

furlough \ ʻfər-ˌlȯ \ n: a weekend pass to go home from jail <went home on a __>

GA \ 'ga \ vb: to be mad at someone <to be __ at a person>

gang war\vb: or **gang warred**: verbal or physical altercation between persons, usu. a verbal argument. < the inmate gang warred with the C.O for losing his property.>

gate gangsta \ 'gāt-gaŋ-stə \ n: an inmate that talks hostile, or bullies behind a closed cell door, but fears a physical altercation <the cowardly __>

GD *(acronym)* Gangsta Disciples <the __ is a gang>

getting money \ 'get-in-mō-nē \ vb: [1]masterbating: [2]to cash a check: [3]stealing: [4]to exercise/workout [4]<Rell was __ in his cell> [4]<was __ in the gym>

gipper \ 'gēp-pər \ n: a homosexual <the proud __>

GLP *(acronym)* General Labor Pool

GP *(acronym)* General Population

green sheet\n: a piece of paper with a decision made by the parole board granting or denying the release of an inmate from prison

gunner \ 'gə-nər \ n: [1]a name that is given to an inmate who masturbates to the site of a female C.O.: [2]freak

---

halk \ 'hälk \ n: [1]jail knife: [2]a shank <the inmate had a __>

herm \ 'hərm \ n: a male homosexual injected with hormones to grow breasts <the confused __ wanted breasts>

himethy\adj: [1]a popular person: [2]that boy: [3]a very important person [3]<because a lot of people showed him attention he started acting like he was himethy>

hole \ 'hold \ n: [1]referring to the R.H.U: [2]restricted housing unit where inmate violators are in 23/ 1-hour lock down [1]<was punished in the __>

homo thug \ n: a gay thug

honkie \ 'hȯn-kē \ n: a white person, usually used derogatorily <the proud __>

hooch \ 'hủch \ n: jail house alcohol <got drunk off __>

hood book \ 'hủd-'bủk \ n: urban novel <read a __>

horse \ 'hȯrs \ n: a corrupted C.O. that brings in contraband for inmates for pay <Katie's __ brought in some cell phones>

husky \ 'həs-kē \ adj: [1]a muscular person: [2]a lot of something [2]<the __ tray>

hut \ ʻhət \ n: a cell <the inmate cleaned his __>

Ice cream cart

.

<u>**it ain't there**   **I**</u>

Ice cream cart \ n: a cart with medication for inmates that are living in restricted housing units brought to them by the nurse

indigent \ ʻin-di-jənt \ adv: [1]having $10 or less in your account for at least 30 days: [2]poor inmate

inmate \ ʻin-ˌmāt \ n: prisoner <the __ was wrongfully accused>

inmatress \ ʻin-ˌmātress \ n: female prisoner <the __ waited on her court date>

institutionalized \ ʻin-ˈsī-tŭ-shon-alized \ adj: being unable to live outside of prison

intercom \ ʻin-tər-ˌkäm \ n: communications system to inform inmates or staff

it ain't there *(phrase)*: a phrase used to say "no", or to let a person down nicely <Rick asked for some money, and his friend said __>

jack \ 'jak \ n: or **jacked**: [1]phone [1]<the inmates waited to use the __> *vb:* [2]to steal something [2]<__ his food>

jailbird \ 'jāl-ˌbərd \ n: [1]one who has a habit of going to jail: [2]institutionalized [1]<the homeless __>

jail house twitter *(phrase)*: the gossip or rumors that's being spread around the jail or prison by inmates or staff <according to the _ we are going to be locked down for two weeks>

jaw \ 'jȯn \ n: [1]anything physical or abstract: [2]homosexual [1]<I like that __ right there>

jeffing \ vb: [1]talking to the police: [2]dry snitching

jerkin rec \ 'jərk-in-rāk \ vb: to interrupt a game or progress <you __ for interrupting our game>

joint \ 'jȯint \ n: [1]anything physical or abstract: [2]homosexual: [3]blade [1]<that __ is nice>

jones \ 'jōnēz \ vb: [1]addiction to heroin: [2]to have a craving for something: [3]heroin [2]<Rick had the __ for cake>

Julee \ 'jǔ-lē \ n: jail house alcohol <the inmate got drunk off __>

kite

.

k-two **K**

---

kite \ 'kit \ n: [1]a letter [1]<sent __ to his family>: [2]tobacco

k-two \ n: [1]deuce: [2]synthetic marijuana [1]<got high off __>

L \ 'el \ n: life sentence

laid an egg \ vb: ¹to pass gas: ²to fart

lango \ 'laŋ-gō \ n: gang code or slang words

Latin Kings \ 'lat-ən-ˈkiŋ \ n: Spanish gang

law library \ 'lō-ˈlī̱ˌbrer-ē \ n: library of legal books in the jail or prison

¹line \ 'līn \ n: a cloth line in the cell used to hang up wet clothes

²line \ n: a rope used for "fishing" to get something from another cell

loligil \ 'lä-li-gē \ n: *(Jamaican Slang)*: penis

loud speaker \ 'laůd_ \ n: intercom used to inform inmates on a block

main line \ n: [1]the chow hall or cafeteria: [2]mess hall

meat gazing\ vb: or **cock gazing**; the act of looking into another persons' cell < he was meat gazing on his way to his hut.>

mess hall \ n: chow hall, main line or cafeteria <the inmates ate in the __>

mo \ n: another term for homosexuals <the happy __>

MS·13 \ n: Hispanic gang

mud \ n: coffee <they drank some __ to stay up>

nickel \ 'nī-kəl \ n: five-year sentence

nigga \ 'nig-a \ n: [1]a common friendly term used amongst persons: [2]a derogatory term used to degrade African Americans [1]<What's up my -?>

nut \ 'nət \ n: a foolish or stupid person <you're a __ Pauly>

nutty\adj: a bad situation or referring to a crazy person

old head \ n: [1]an older guy one may seek wisdom from: [2]a mentor (as an O.G)

old-timer \ n: [1]an old head: [2]an old person doing a life sentence: [3]a veteran in prison

on da muscle\vb: or **from da muscle**: [1]taking care of one's self: [2]self reliance: [3]by myself

[3]<I'm doing this bid from da muscle>

on (··) top \ vb: [1]to annoy someone, or to become a nuisance to someone: [2]to pursue a person, usually for an unpaid debt

[1]<my friend was on my top when I went to the yard>

[2]<I'm on his top when I see him, I need my money!>

*(replace underscore with a possessive noun or pronoun, my, her, their, etc.)

paper work \ n: court papers

parie \ 'pär-ē \ n: [1]friend: [2]walkie

parole\n: the privilege of an inmate being released from prison after serving a minimum sentence and then the remainder on supervision on the street

parole board\n: a nine-member panel responsible for the release or denial of an inmate in prison *(varies in different regions)

P.C. *(acronym)* \ protective custody

pecker wood \ n: white supremacist group

phone boss\n: an inmate who controls a certain phone on the block in which other inmates must go through him to get on the phone

phone bully\n: an inmate who intimidate others by not letting them get on the phone or by telling them how much time they can spend on the phone

poke up \ vb: or **poked up**: to stab someone <to get __>

popin fly \ vb: to talk disrespectfully to a person

population \ ˌpü·pyə-'lā-shən \ n: general inmate housing, not P.C or the hole, etc.

pound \ vb: fist bump or to give dap <gave his friend a __>

Prison clingy \ vb: emotionally clinging to any contact outside of prison as a point of stability

programs \ n: rehabilitative course for inmates

pruno \ 'prü-nō \ n: jail house alcohol <he got drunk off __>

P Stone Rangers \ n: African American gang

punk \ n: [1]homosexual: [2]joint: [3]fag

pussy \ n: refers to the male butt hole

P.V. *(acronym)* parole violation

quarter

.

<u>Quarter</u>   **Q**

quarter \ n: twenty-five-year sentence

rack in \ 'rak- \ vb: return your cell <the C.O. told the inmates to __>

ramming \ 'ram-iŋ \ vb: yelling in a loud aggressive tone <John started __ after he found out his friend was lying>

rappy \ 'ra-pē \ n: co-defendant in a criminal case

razor and comb \ n: haircut given by another inmate <O got a fresh __ before his visit>

reck \ 'rek \ [1]n: [1]recreational activities [1]<the inmates enjoyed their __>: [2]vb: [2]fighting [2]<Bob was recking the guard>

reck chasing \ 'rek_ \ vb: looking for trouble <the new inmate was __ so that he could fit in>

recreation \ ˌre-krē-ā-shən \ vb: activity outside the cell <the inmate enjoyed their __>

red dragon \ 'red-dra-gən \ n: [1]gay or homosexual: [2]joint: [3]gipper

reroll \ 'ri-rō \ n: leftover tobacco used to make new cigarettes <Tim was smoking a __ cigarette>

RHU (acronym) \ restricted housing unit

roadie \ 'rō-dē \ n: [1]a friend: [2]a walkie: [3]homie <his __ took care of his beef>

roadio \ 'rō-dē-ō \ vb: [1]doing a sentence in jail or prison: [2]a trip to jail: [3]experience in prison [1]<he did a five year __>

roll up \ 'rōl_ \ n: [1]a cigarette: [2]a caddie: [3]buck horn <smoked a __>

roofed \vb: receiving a long prison sentence

run down\vb: or **ran down**: [1]an inmate being searched by a c.o.: [2]to rob someone [1]<The c.o. ran down on 37 cell>[2]<The inmate ran down on someone for his commissary>

sally port

.

sally port \ n: area between the block and the entrance/exit in a jail or prison

sarge \ n: a correction officer under a captain, but superior to a regular C.O.

sauced up \ 'sȯs-ed_ \ adj: [1]experienced in the street life: [2]high or drunk [1]<the __ inmate>

scrape \ 'sk-'rāp \ n: rape <got charged with __>

send or **sent** \ vb: referring to someone being killed <Bill got sent>

settle da scores \ vb: [1]revenge: [2]to get even with someone: [3]truce

[1]**shank** \ n: [1]a makeshift stabbing weapon: [2]banger [1]<used a __>

[2]**shank** \ vb: [1]to shank: [2]to stab or to get stabbed: **shanked** <got shanked>

shank down \ vb: the raiding of an inmate's cell <the entire jail had a __>

sha moody \ 'sha-'mü-dē \ n: gay; homosexual

sheets and towels \ adj: phrase used by the Co.'s to inform the inmates that it's time to change your sheets and towels <__ means it's time to get clean sheets and towels for the week> *may be different in other prisons

shot caller \ n: [1]the leader of a gang <the __ had someone shanked>: [2]boss

shower sheet \ n: a sheet used as a shower curtain (in some jails or prison they don't have curtains or doors on the showers) <used the ___ to cover the shower>

sick \ adj: stressing or sad <Mike was ___ when he didn't get mail for the day>

singing \ 'sit-in \ vb: [1]snitching: [2]telling: [3]ratting [1]<his co-defendant was ___ during the trial>

skin heads \ n: white supremacist group

skittles \ 'skit-tləs \ n: medication

slide \ 'slīd \ n: [1]an object used for fishing: *(see fishing)* [1]<he used a ___ to retrieve his book from another cell>: [2]to leave

sling shots \ 'sliŋ- \ n: [1]briefs: [2]supermans

smash \ 'smash \ vb: [1]referring to taking a dump: [2]to have sex with; **smashed** [1]<he took a ___> [2]<he smashed a girl>

smut jawn \ 'smət-'jȯn \ n: nude pictures <masturbated to the ___s>

soapboxing \ 'sōp-ˌbäksiŋ \ adj: a long or repetitive speech <a ___ speech>

soups \ süps \ n: usually ramen noodle soup or any noodle soups (main product in a chi chi)

spin artist \ 'spin_' \ n: [1]a person that tries to get one over on other people: [2]trickster <the crafty ___>

squalae \ 'skwä-lā \ n: a phrase used by inmates to alert each other when a C.O. is coming near a cell or on a block, where illegal activities are being conducted

square \ 'skwers \ n: [1]buck horn: [2]cigarette <smoked a ___>

stamp \ 'stamp \ n: **stamped**: tattoo <had his girlfriend's name stamped on his arm>

stash \ 'stash \ n: a hiding place <hide his pictures in his __>

steeling \ 'stēl·in \ vb: [1]to masturbate: [2]jack off: [3]cash a check: [4]cashing out

stick \ 'stik \ n: [1]cigarette: [2]buck horn [3]square <smoked a __>

stinger \ 'stiŋ-ər \ n: [1]an extension cord attached to a nail clipper or a piece of metal, used to cook a meal: [2]referring to a small cigarette or the butt of one [1]<used a __ to boil some water in his cell>

stinger hawk \ n: an inmate scavenger collecting cigarette butts from the ground or trash can

strapped up\adv: an inmate having his state boots on and ready to fight: one armed with a weapon ready to use it

<the inmate strapped up before leaving his cell

stress box \ 'stres_ \ n: person that is always worried, depressed, or stressing

stress boxing \ vb: to worry

sucka duck \ vb: to hide out in your cell so you won't get in trouble bcforc being released from prison

super mans \ n: [1]briefs: [2]sling shots

tango blast \ 'taŋ-gō-'blast \ n: Hispanic gang

tap out \ 'tap_ \ vb: [1]to give up: [2]an inmate checking into P.C. *(protective custody)*: **tapped out** [1]<the inmate tapped out because he was scared>

the man \ 'thə_ \ n: referring to the government (i.e. police or C.O.) <__ is coming>

thuging it \ 'thə-in_ \ vb: to handle suffering with a sense of dignity <I don't have any snacks so I'm __>

tick \ 'tik \ n: [1]a sentence in prison or jail: [2]time 1<he got a lot of __>

ticket\n: [1]a write up: [2]gambling ticket

[1]<Got a _ from the c.o.> [2]<played a _>

time \ 'tīm \ n: [1]tick: [2]a sentence in prison or jail <his brother was doing __ upstate>

tipping \ 'tip-iŋ \ vb: [1]being disrespectful: [2]outtapocket <the inmate was __ on the C.O.>

top \ vb: **on (··) top**: [1]to annoy someone: *(syn)* [2]sweat <get off my __>

TP *(acronym)* toilet paper

trade \ n: [1]a male who dates a transsexual: [2]booty bandit

trays \ n: [1]main line: [2]chow time <the C.O. said "__" when it was time to eat>

tree jumper \ n: [1]a homosexual: [2]child molester <Darran was a __>

trustie \n: an inmate that can work in commonly restricted areas in the jail\prison

tryin a catch \ 'trī-inä_ \ vb: flirting with the same sex to see if one might be gay <the gay guy was __>

turkey time \ adj: sneaky <the man was on __>

turned out \ 'tərn·ed_ \ vb: [1]to do something against one's morals (Ex. a non-homosexual practicing homosexuality): [2]to lose control

turn key \ n: correction officer

[1]**twist** \ n: [1]the restricted housing unit: [2]the bucket: [3]the hole <he went to the __>

[2]**twist** \ vb: to get in trouble <he got caught up in the __>

unit \ n: [1]the block: [2]a section of the block where inmates live (ex. section A or B)

up north \ n: [1]state prison: [2]up top

up-top \ n: [1]state prison: [2]up north: [3]used in the feds, referring to the hole (see hole)

.

vent hustle \ vb: **-hustling**: to secretly listen to a conversation through the cell's ventilation system (in jail/prison, each cell is connected to the same ventilation system)

vent hustler \ 'vent- \ n: a person who vent hustles casually to interrupt enjoyment or to be nosy

V·I \ n: a visit <the inmate went on his __>

viking \ n: [1]a dirty or nasty person: [2]unclean

violation \ n: parole violation <the inmate was in jail on a __>

wack \ 'wak \ n: [1]shank: [2]a knife or sharp object: [3]lame [1]<a sharp __>[3]<that joke was __>

wake up \ 'wāk _ \ n: [1]the day of release: [2]a morning ritual (coffee, cig., etc.) [1]<the inmate was happy on his __>

walkie \ ˌwȯ-kē \ n: a person who walks with his friend <my __ walked with me to lunch>

wamming \ 'wäm-in \ n: a strong odor <that fart was __>

wat car you in \ phrase \ what gang are you in? <__?>

whites \ 'hwītz \ n: underclothes (ex. t-shirts, socks, briefs, boxers, or sheets and towels) <changed his __>

wic \ 'wik \ n: a piece of paper rolled up and lit that is used as a lighter <used a __ to lite his smoke>

wiggler \ 'wi-glər \ n: [1]a child molester: [2]tree jumper: [3]chomo

window licker \ n: [1]a mentally challenged person: [2]a retarded person

work \ n: [1]a penis: [2]pipe: [3]manns: [4]dick [1]<put a condom on his __>

worker \ n: an inmate with a job, usually a block job <the __ swept the floor>

writ \ 'rit \ vb: a state inmate leaving to go to court <went on __>

write-up \ n: a disciplinary misconduct that can stop an inmate's release <the inmate received a __ for fighting>

yard

.

<u>**you heard me**</u>   **Y**

yard \ n: the prison yard

you heard me \ *phrase* \ you understand

Zata

.

Zata   **Z**

Zata \ 'zå-tå \ n: Hispanic gang

STREET

SLANG

ah hit \vb: a contract killing

aight \ 'I-hight \ adj: ¹another way to say all right or ok: ²to agree with: ³all day

all dat \ 'ol·da-t \ adj: something beautiful to the eye or excellent

all da way live *(phrase)*: hype

all da way up *(phrase)*: ¹rich, successful: ²above and beyond: ³to the extreme: ⁴drunk or high: ⁵all the way live

all day \ adv: ¹an expression of agreement (usually yes): ²aight <do you like cake? __>

all the way *(phrase)*: ¹yes: ²to finish something

amped up \ 'amp-ed·op \ vb: ¹excited or energized: ²hyper active or happy: ³hype: ⁴all da way live ¹<the crowd was __>

angel dust \ 'an-jel·dest \ n: ¹PCP: ²turbo: ³crack: ⁴cocaine

ASAP *(acronym)*: as soon as possible

as shit \ əz-sh-it \ adv: a phrase used to exaggerate something <Tom was doing 120mph on the highway, he is crazy __!>

¹ass \ 'as \ adj: someone who can't properly do something or is bad at it <Bill is __ at poker> n: buttocks, usually referring to a female's butt <she has a nice __>

²ass \ vb: referring to having sexual intercourse <Ray just got some __ from his girlfriend>

Axe to grind \ vb: have an axe to grind: ¹something to complain about: ²selfish reason for doing something: ³ulterior motive ¹<Jim had an __ with his man>

AYO \ 'a-yō\ [1]used to call attention to or to indicate attentiveness: [2] to express affirmation [1]<the bartender was not paying attention, so he said __ to get his attention>

B

.

<u>**ball**</u>   <u>**B**</u>

B \ 'be \ n: referring to a person like a cousin or friend <what's up __?>

baby dad \n: or **baby father**: referring to the father of a child

baby mom \n: or **baby momma** or **baby mother**: referring to the mother of a child

Babylon \ 'bäb-i-lan \ adj: [1]places and people of wickedness, and depression: [2]police [1]<__ will not prosper>

back at it \ 'bak- 'ät- 'it \ vb: to do something that you didn't do in a while <he came out of retirement and now is __>

badd \ 'bad \ adj: [1]beautiful; [2]superbad: [3]dime: [4]on fleek [1]<She is __>

badd bitch \ 'bad- 'bich \ adj: [1]a beautiful female with nice curves and high confidence: (syn) [2]dime [1]<she is a __>

bad mon \ bäd- 'man \ adj: a ruthless man <Jeff is a __>

bad money \ 'bad- 'məē \ adj: [1]not trustworthy: [2]referring to a snitch or a robber <he is __>

babbitt \ 'bä-bit \ n: low quality drugs

ba·dun·ka·dunk \ 'bá-donk-ka-dank \ n: [1]a buttock: [2]ass: [3]donkey; [4]to compliment or exaggerate a person's butt [1]<Damn! She got a __>

bag \ 'bag \ vb: bagged: [1]to acquire something: [2]to be arrested [1]<__ the girl> [2]<got __>

ball or **balling** \ vb: [1]flashy: [2]successful or rich: [3]to start a game[1]<He was balling in his jewelry.>

bananas \ adv: [1]crazy: [2]trippin: [3]shot out: [4]hot

bands \ n: stacks of a thousand dollars

bang \ vb: **banged**: [1]to have sexual intercourse: [2]smash: [3]hit: [4] to defend a gang or a set, usually by violence

banging \ 'baŋ-ing \ adj: [1]something admirable or admired: *(syn)* [2]excellent: [3]fly: [4]dope: [5]on fleek [1]<a __ car>

bang out \ 'baŋ-aůt \ vb: or **bang-ed out**: [1]to crash a car: [2]to stab or being stabbed [1]<banged out his car> [2]<Pater got banged out>

barking up the wrong tree \ vb: [1]picking a fight or a dispute with a more advantaged person: [2]taking on something that one cannot handle [1]<Allis was __>

battery in his back \ vb: [1]to instigate: *(syn)* [2]egging on: [3]flunky <he put a __ to rob the bank>

batty boy \n: or **batty man** *(Jamaican Slang)*: a homosexual

beaver \ 'bē-vər \ n: slang for vagina <every girl has a __>

Becky \ 'bek-ē \ n: [1]referring to a white female; vb: [2]oral sex: *(syn)* [3]head: [4]top: [5]chopper [2]<Jen likes to give __>

be easy \ 'be- 'ē-zē \ n: [1]a concluding remark at parting: [2] take care [1]<__ Ray, see you tomorrow>

beef \ 'bēf \ vb: **beefing**: [1]verbal or physical altercation: *(syn)* [2]throwing shade: [3]controversy [1]<Tupac and Biggie had the biggest __ of all time>

bees \ 'bē-z \ n: [1]the police: *(syn)* [2]Five·O: [3]pigs: [4]the boys

B.F *(acronym)* best friend or boyfriend

B.F.F *(acronym)* best female friend

biddy \ 'bi-dē \ n: **biddies**: a young female <Molly and her __ went to the movies>

big-timer \ 'big-tim-ər \ n: [1]a rich successful person: *(syn)* [3]big homie: [3]baller: [4]boss

bill gates \ 'bil- 'gāts \ vb: to take advantage of someone's idea <to __ someone>

[1]**birds** \ 'bərd-s \ n: [1]multiple kilos of cocaine: *(syn)* [2]bricks [1]<he hid the __ in his trunk>

[2]**bird** \ adj: an unattractive person, usually referring to a female <she's a __>

bisquet \ 'bisk-ēt \ n: slang for a person's head containing the brain <the ball hit him in his __>

bitch \ 'bich \ n: **bitchies**: a girl <I like that __ over there>

bite \ 'bīt \ vb: biting \ -tin \: [1]to copy a person's style: [2]to imitate [1]<Tommy was __ing how his brother dressed>

black Friday \n: the day after thanksgiving, where everything is on sale at half price and people go shopping

blaze \ 'blāz \ vb: **blazed**: **blazing**: [1]to smoke: [2]being high from smoking [1]<they were about to __> [2]<they were __ed>

block \ 'bläk \ n: [1]neighborhood street with large building divided into separate units: [2]a row of homes or shops on a street [1]<they were chilling on the __>

block or mo \ adj: [1]a phrase used to describe an unattractive female or male:[2]she only looks good from a block or more [1]<she's a __>

blood\n: [1]a gang: [2]a Jamaican usu. referred to as 'blood'

blood drop \ -dräp \ n: A Blood member's baby <Ronny's newborn was considered a __ because he was a member of the Bloods>

bloodette \ -ēt \ n: a female Blood member: see **Bloods** <there are not many __ in gangs>

blow up \ vb: to get popular or to gain fame

blue \ 'blü \ adj: sad or depressing <he's feeling __>

Blue rag \ - 'rag \ n: nickname for the Crips gang <he's a __>

blunt \ 'blənt \ n: weed rolled in a cigar wrapper ready to smoke <they smoked a __>

B.M *(acronym)* baby mother

boatload \ 'bōt-lōd \ adv: [1]having a lot of something: [2]bookoo [1]<he has a __ of money>

bobble head \ 'bäbəl- 'hed \ n: a nickname for a female that loves to give oral pleasures <she's a __>

body \ 'bä-dē \ adj: **bodied**: [1]referring to a dead body: vb [2]referring to someone being killed or murdered: *(syn)* [3]off'ed: [4]x'd out [1]<a __ on the floor> [2]<he got __ied yesterday>

body count \ - 'kaůnt \ adv: the number of sexual partners had or the number of murders one committed <what's your __?>

body shaming \ adj: [1]negative comments made about a person's size or weight: [2]fat shaming

bom·bo·clat \ ' ˌbōm- ˌbō-clät \ adj: [1]a derogatory term used in grief or anger: [2]fxxk

bomb shell \ 'bäm- ˌshell \ n: a secret discovered that causes one to be completely upset <what a __>

bone \ 'bōn \ vb: **boned**: **boning**: ¹referring to having sex: *(syn)* ²smash ¹<he __ed her>

boner \ 'bōnər \ vb: having an erection <he had a __ when he saw her naked>

bones \ -z \ n: ¹money: *(syn)* ²dow: ³cheese: ⁴bread: ⁵paper ¹<he was counting his __>

boo \ 'bü \ n: ¹affectionate term used by significant other towards each other: ²pet name ¹ <hi __>

booed up \ adv :¹intimately together with a person: ²cuddling ¹<they were _ at the movie theater.>

boogy \ 'bü -jē \ adj: conceited <__attitude>

boo koo \ 'bü-kü \ adj: ¹abundance: ²boatload ¹<Bill Gates has a __ load of money>

boo love \ adv: or **boo loved** or **boo loving**: an affectionate or intimate conversation or strong emotion between significant others <Hey baby you are so pretty and sweet, was said while they boo loved on the phone.>

boost \ 'büst \ vb: boosted: to steal, usually a car

boot licker \ adj: a person who volunteers himself or volunteers to undertake a service or duty to gain authority

booty \ n: ¹sex: ²butt: ³badunkadunk: ⁴ass: ⁵donkey ¹<I just got some __> ²<she got a nice __>

booty call \ vb: a phone call resulting in persons having sex, usually a late-night phone call <she made a late night __>

booty·lic·lous \ 'bü-tē-lē-shē-ous \ adj: ¹badunkadunk; ²seductive: ³sexy: ²<she is so __>

booty·o·logy \-lƏ-jē\ n: ¹the ideology of female sexuality: ²dealing with sexuality

boss \'bäs \ n: the leader or manager of a particular group or organization <Mike is the __ of his music group>

boss status \ 'bäs- 'stā-təs \ n: ¹high esteem for a boss in the eyes of others or of the law: ²leadership status: ³highest level of leadership <he's __>

bot \' bät \ n: ¹slang name to call a friend: *(syn)* ²son: ³cuz: ⁴bro: ⁵nigga, etc. ²<what's up __>

bottom line \vb: ¹to get to the point of a situation: ²conclusion of an argument ¹<So let's get to the __ of this.> ²<end of the conversation __>

boul \'bül \ n: ¹referring to a male friend: *(syn)* ²bot: ³son: ⁴cuz: ⁵bro: ⁶nigga ¹<what's up __>

boulder \ ˌbōl-dər \ n: slang for crack rocks <the drug dealer sold some __ to an undercover>

bounce \ 'baůns \ vb: ¹to leave: ²to dip ¹<I'm about to __>

bow cat\ n: *(Jamaican Slang)*: a person who gives oral sex, usu. a man but can also be a woman

bowdit \ 'baů-dēt \ n: ¹promiscuous girl: ²smut: ³bout that life ¹<she's a __>

box \ 'bäks \ n: ¹vagina: ²casket ¹<a woman's __> ²<buried in a __>; vb: ³to fight

brain \ vb: ¹oral sex: ²head: ³top ¹<she gave him some __>

break bread \'brāk-bred \ vb: **breaking bread**; **broke bread**: to share <He broke bread with his family.>

bread \ 'bred \ n: [1]money: (syn) [2]cheese: [3]gwap: [4]chedder: [5]bones: [6]paper: [7]dow: [8]mula: [9]cake (similar slang terms for money) <he spent some __ on his car>

breeds \ 'brēds \ n: biker gang originated in New Jersey

brick \ 'brik \ n: one kilo of cocaine <he sold the undercover police officer a __>

brink \ 'briŋk \ adj: cold <it was __ outside>

bro \ 'brō \ n: [1]brother: [2]referring to a friend: *(syn)* [3]son: [4]cuz: [5]nigga [1]<what's up __>

broad \ 'bròd \ n: [1]a girl: [2]an unmarried female: *(syn)* [3]bitch: [4]chick

browdy \ 'brō-dē \ vb: **browdied**: [1]to take away by force or to steal something from someone: [2]to fall [1]<he __ the man for his money> [2]<he took __>

brownie points \ n: [1]favor, respect, or appreciation with authority figures: [2]to gain favor by doing something for a person <Jerry worked overtime for his boss to gain __>

brown nose \ vb: **brown-nosing**: to automatically agree with authority figures to gain favor

brown noser \ n: one who brown noses

brown Pride \ n: Hispanic gang originated in Nashville

BS *(acronym)*: bull shit

buck \ 'bək \ n: [1]referring to a young male: *(syn)* [2]youngin: [3]young buck

bucket \ adv: basketball term used when a shot has been made

buck fifty \ - 'fif-tē \ vb: referring to a person getting sliced, usually requiring 150 stitches *(gang term)* <he gave his enemy a __>

buddy \ bə-dē \ n: [1]friend or companion: [2]a penis [1]<what's up __>

bugaboo \ 'bə-gə- 'bü \ adj: [1]a person who annoys by free-loading off others: [2]lame [1]<he's a __>

bugging \ 'bəg-gin \ vb: [1]to annoy: *(syn)* [2]trippin: [3]outta pocket [1]<the flight attendant was __>

bull \ 'bůl \ n: [1]nonsense: [2]vb: to inform someone that you know they are lying: [3]BS [1]<that's __>

bum \ 'bəm \ adj: a poor homeless person who spends time unemployed wandering or devotes time on recreational activities <she's a __>

bundle \ 'bən-dəl \ n: 13 bags of any drugs, bagged up and ready to sell, usually dope <the drug dealer sold two __s>

bunz \ 'bən-z \ n: [1]buttox: *(syn)* [2]ass: [3]booty: [4]cake: [5]badunkadunk: etc. [3]<she got some nice __>

burn \ 'bərn \ vb: **burned**: [1]not paying someone their due: [2]to steal [1]<Ray burned his friend.> [2]<__ for money>

burned-out \ vb: **burning out**: [1]tired (ex. tired from doing something): [2]to make someone tired [1]<Tim was __ after the game>

burner \ 'bər-ner \ n: [1]a gun: [2]an untraceable cell phone [1]<the police officer had a new __>

burning \ 'bər-in \ vb: a person infected with an STD <she was __, so she went to the doctor>

burnout \ n: an annoying person <my friend can be a real __ something>

bury the hatchet \ 'ber-ē-thə-'ha'chət \ vb: to come to a state of peace with a person whom one was at odds with <after years of war, they buried the hatchet>

buss on \ 'bəs-on \ vb: **bussed on**; **bussing on**; [1]to make fun of someone or embarrass them: *(syn)* [2]grinding up: [3]to rip on [1]<they bussed on the boy with the big ears>

buss a lick \vb: to go on a robbery or to buss a trap

buss a trap \ 'bəs-əs-trap \ vb: [1]to make a drug sale: *(syn)* [2]trappin: [3]slinging [1]<he __ to the fiend>

buss your chops \ 'bəs- 'yǔr-chap-z \ vb: [1]to set a person straight by surprise information: [2]to put a person in check: bussed your chops: [3]to give someone a hard time [1]<he bussed his chops>

busta \ 'best-a \ adj: [1]a punk: *(syn)* [2]loser: [3]lame person: [4]fiend [1]<the scared __>

butt \ 'but \ n: the end part of a cigar or weed split <he smoked the cigar all the way to the __>

butta head \ 'bət-tā- hed \ adj: [1]everything looks good but her head: [2]a phrase used to describe a person with an attractive body and an unattractive face [1]<she's a __>

butters \ 'bə-ter-z \ n: nickname for Timberland boots <he just bought a new pair of __>

bye Felicia \ *phrase*: [1]dismissing a female: [2]subject you don't care about: [3]get out of here: [4]who cares

bye Tyrone \ *phrase*: [1]dismissing a male you don't care for: [2]irrelevant male: [3]who cares

by the book \ *phrase*: done strictly by the rules

cake \ 'kāk \ n: [1]money: *(syn)* [2]butt: [3]booty: [4]ass: [5]buttox: [6]donkey: [7]monkey etc. [1]<he spent a lot of __ on the car> [2]<she has a nice __>

cakewalk \ 'kāk-wȯk \ adv: anything easily done <playing this game is a __ to me>

came up \ 'kām-əp \ vb: **come up**: [1]getting successful after a life or period of poverty: [2]come up [1]<he __ off his book deal>

can \ n: **the can**: [1]the bathroom: [2]referring to jail

candy paint \ 'kan-dē-pānt \ adj: bright colors on cars <I like the __ on that car>

cannon \ 'ka-nən \ n: [1]young ruthless person: *(syn)* [2]thug: [3]goon [1]<he's a __>

cap up \ 'kap-əp \: **capped up**: [1]to instigate: [2]to lie [1]<he capped up the man to jump> [2]<he tried to cap up the police officers>

cat \ n: [1]a cigarette: [2]a women's vagina: [3]referring to a male: [4]bro: [5]cuz: [6]B [1]<he sneaked an __ into the no smoking building.> [2]<she keeps her __ clean> [3]<that __ just got out of jail.>

catcall \ vb; **catcalled**; **catcalling**: random flirtatious remarks towards a female that one wants to date <cat called the pretty lady>

cat daddy \ 'kat-'da-dē \ n: the name of a dance

cat in a hat \ n: [1]a snitch: [2]rat: [3]informer <your boy is a __>

check \ 'chek \ vb: [1]to set the record straight with a person: n: [2]money [1]<he had to __ his lawyer>

checked \ chek-ed \ vb: referring to someone dead <his grandmother just __>

cheese \ ¹chēz \ n: ¹money: ²bread: ³cake: ⁴dow: ⁵mula ¹<spent his
__>

cherry-picking \ ʻcher-ē-ˈpik-iŋ \ vb: ¹waiting at the top of the key
in the basketball game for an easy shot: ²waiting for something to
come easy

chewy \ ʻchü- ē \ vb: ¹getting oral sex: ²head: ³brain: ⁴top: ⁵chopper
<she gave him some __>

chick \ ʻchik \ n: woman or girl <pretty__>

chicken \ ʻchi-kən \ n: ¹small amount of cocaine: ²money: ³dow:
⁴cheese: ⁵bread: ⁶cake ¹<he sold some __ to the fiend> ²<he spent his
__>

chicken head \ - ʻhed \ adj: ¹an uneducated nasty woman or girl:
²clucker: ³ghetto

chicken noodle soup \ - ʻnu-dəl-ˈsüp \ n: name of a dance

chill \ ʻchil \ vb: **chilling**; ¹to relax: ²to hang out <to __>

chill out \ - ʻaut \ vb: ¹to rebuke someone: ²telling someone to stop
being annoying ²<she told the kids to __ because they were being too
loud>

chip on your shoulder \ vb: ¹something bothering a person causing
one to be angry: ²withholding from addressing a problem

chipped \ ʻchip-ed \ vb: referring to someone being killed <got __>

chirp \ ʻchərp \ vb: ¹to leave: ²bounce: chirped; ³being talkative
¹<I'm about to __ out of here> ³<he __ too much>

chop it up \ vb: ¹to sit down and talk with a person: ²conversation
<the __ together>

chopped \ 'chäp-ed \ vb: [1]mistake: [2]the wrong idea [2]<he got me __>

chopper \ 'chä-pər \ n: an assault rifle, usually an AK47

chump \ 'chə-mē \ n: a cowardly person

chumped \ vb: to be embarrassed or bullied by someone <Tom got __ by the school bully>

C.I. \ *abbr*: confidential informant

clap \ 'kläp \ n: an STD, usually gonorrhea

clash in \ 'klåsh-in \ adv: [1]wearing clothes that don't match: [2]miss match <wearing a pink shirt and yellow pants would be considered __>

clique \ 'klēk \ n: [1]social group that hangs together and are usually engaged in criminal activities: [2]a gang

clown \ 'klaůn \ n: a foolish person

clucker \ 'klō- ker \ adj: [1]chickenhead: [2]bird

club banger \ 'kləb-'ban-er \ n: a hit song that club goers enjoy hearing in the club <that song is __>

Cock blocking \ 'käk-'bäk-in \ adj: [1]a person that stops two people from having sexual intercourse: [2]hating [1]<her friend was __ so hard last night that I didn't smash>

coke \ 'kōk \ n: cocaine <snorted __>

cold turkey \ 'kōld-'tər-kē \ vb: stopping something suddenly without warning, usually a habit <he quit __>

come up \ 'kəm-'əp \ vb: [1]to gain new opportunity or to increase in success: [2]came up [1]<that's a major __>

coming at my neck \ vb: [1]to argue: [2]to attack someone verbally [1]<my girlfriend was __ all night>

coming out\vb: or **came out** or **coming out of the closet** or **came out of the closet**: admitting that one is homosexual or transgender

commando \ 'kə-'man-dō \ vb: not wearing underwear <going __>

connect \ 'kə-nekt \ n: [1]supplier: [2]the plug: [3]distributor [1]<he got his drugs from his __>

cool points \ 'kul-'pȯintz \ n: [1]a mental note of likeable traits (ex. cool points are used to rank how likeable a person is in another person's point of view): [2]street creds [1]<she gave him __ for opening her door>

coon \ 'kun \ n: a derogatory term used to insult African Americans <you __!>

cop \ 'käp \ vb: to purchase or receive some-thing: copped <he copped a new house>

Cop a plee \ vb: **copped a plee**; **copping a plee**; [1]to ask for mercy: [2]to tap out [1]<he copped a plee when he knew he was losing>

cornball \ 'kȯrn-ˌbȯl \ n: [1]a lame person: [2]a corny person [2]<some people are really __s>

corny \ 'kȯrn-ē \ adj: something boring or lame (ex. a person or thing) <playing golf is so __>

co-sign \ vb: **co-signed**; **co-signing**; [1]to go along with or agree with someone: [2]to vouch for someone [1]<__his friend in the argument>

crack \ 'krak \ n: [1]cocaine in rock form: [2]ready rock: [3]hard <he sold __ to an undercover>

cracked \ 'krāk-ed \ vb: to punch someone in the face <he __ him in the face>

crackin \ 'krak-in \ vb: or **crackin-on** [1]exciting: [2]amped up: [3]turned up: [4]to make fun of someone [1]<the party was __> [2]<*cracked on* his friend.>

crack head \ 'krak-hed \ n: a person addicted to crack or other hard drugs <gave the drugs to the __>

crash dummy \ 'krash-'də-mē \ n: a person that is willing to do something reckless for someone else's cause at any moment <Tom used his friend like a __>

[1]**cream** \ 'krēm \ n: [1]money: [2]cheese: [3]break: [4]cake: [6]gwap, etc. [1]<spent __ on a brand-new watch.>

[2]**cream** *(acronym)* \ cash rules everything around me

Cream of da crop \ adj: [1]a well respected wealthy person: [2]the best of something [2]<Jen is the __ at bowling>

creepin \ 'krēp-in \ vb: [1]cheating: [2]sneaking around <she caught her man __>

crew \ 'krü \ n: [1]clique: [2]social group that works and plays together [1]<Ray loves his __>

crib \ 'krib \ n: [1]house: [2]spot [1]<she went to his __>

crop dust \ 'kräp-'dəst \ n: the odor of a fart left behind by someone that just farted passing by <he left his __ when he walked by>

cross \ 'kròs \ vb: **crossed**: [1]to betray someone: [2]to get angry with someone [1]<he crossed his friend by snitching on him> [2]<she got her husband __ when she came home late>

crunk \ 'krȯnk \ vb: [1]wild looking to fight or wild looking for excitement: [2]amped up: [3]turned up: [4]excited <the par-ty was __>

crusty \ 'krəs-tē \ adj: [1]pale or referring to dry or ashy skin: [2]dirty <the __ bum>

C.T.F.U. *(acronym)* \ cracking the fxxk up

cuffing \ 'kəf-in \ vb: **cuffed**: being overly protective of a spouse <he was cuffing his wife by not letting her go to the club>

cum \ 'kəm \ vb: **cumin**: [1]to ejaculate sperm: [2]to climax: [3]to orgasm: [4]bus a nut [1]<she told her boyfriend to __ inside her so that she could have a baby>

cum bucket\n: [1]a whore or prostitute: [2]referring to the mouth or anal cavity: [3]vagina

cut \ 'kət \ vb: **cutting**: to have sexual intercourse

cuz \ 'kōz \ n: friend or brother or in referring to a random person <what's up __?>

Cyber Monday\n: the first Monday after thanksgiving where everything on the internet is on sale half priced and people go shopping

dab \ 'däb \ adv: a pose where your head is bowed, and your hands are up at a 45-degree angle, created by football player Cam Newton

da butter fly \ 'dā-'bə-tər-flī \ n: the name of a dance <do __>

da game \ 'dā-'gām \ n: referring to the music industry or the streets, usually the rap game or the hustling game <a lot of people try to get in __>

dapper \adj: [1]nicely dressed: [2]fresh [1]<My dress game is dapper!>

daps \ 'dāpz \ vb: to fist bump or to shake one's hand <he gave his friend __>

da sky the limit *(phrase)*: a motivational phrase meaning you can be or do anything you put your mind to <Kim was wondering if she should write a book and then her dad said "__">

dating pool \ 'dāt-in-pül \ n: the people available for dating in a given area <after her break up, she went back into the __>

dats crazy \ 'datz-'krāzē \ adj: unbelievable, unimaginable <they landed on the moon, __>

dat way \ vb: [1]a phrase used to exaggerate a statement: [2]to overstate: [3]a phrase used to get rid of someone who is annoying [1]<I just made a million dollars, yes __!> [2]<I went to Jamaica and had so much fun, __!> [3]<go __>

dawg\ 'dog \ n: or **dog**: a male or female friend, usually male <what's up __?>

D boy \ 'dē-bȯi \ n: [1]a drug dealer: [2]dope boy: [3]drug boy [1]<the __ had a lot of money>

dead\vb: **deaded**; **dead dat**; **deaded dat**: [1]to end a verbal or physical alteration or argument abruptly by way of proof: [2]to put an end to something quickly: [3]to kill someone [1]<Jeff deaded the argument >

[2]<I just found out my girlfriend is stealing from me, I'm going to dead dat, the relationship.>

deep

.

diesel

deep \ 'dēp \ vb: [1]an intense situation: [2]something complex [1]<that story was __>

deuces \ düs-ēz \ vb: duces: [1]good bye: [2]a sign of peace with the index finger and middle finger: [3]two

[1]**dicked** \ adj: [1]messed up or to wreck something (i.e. sneakers): [2]dogged: [3]ugly [3]<he was wearing __ shoes> [1]<he __ his shoe>

Dick head \ adj: a stupid or silly person

[1]**diddy bop** \ vb: to walk with a swag

[2]**diddy bop** \ n: the name of a dance <she loves my __>

did it \ 'dīd-ēt \ vb: **doing it**; **to do it**: [1]to have sex: [2]swag: [3]hit [1]<when they __, she got pregnant> [2]<you doing it girl>

dime \ 'dīm \ n: [1]a pretty girl: [2]ten dollars' worth of drugs or referring to the number ten [1]<she is a __> [2]<he bought a __>

dip \ 'dip \ vb: **dipped**: to leave or to run away fast <he __ed early>

dipper \ dip-pər \ n: a cigarette dipped in PCP <he got high off a __>

dirty \ n: **dirty south**: the southern part of the United States, usually referring to the hood.

dirty money \ n: [1]money obtained illegally: [2]drug money [1]<they did not want to spend the __>

diesel \ 'dī-sel \ n: [1]high quality weed: [2]dank <the Rastas smoked __>

.

Donny Brasco

diss \ ʻdis \ vb: to insult a person: **dissed** <she dissed her boyfriend for another man>

D.I.Y. *(acronym)* do it yourself

D.L. *(acronym)* down low

D.M. *(acronym)* direct message

D mack \ ʻdē-ˈmak \ n: **d macking**: the name of a dance

doe \ ʻdō \ n: ¹a friend: ²dawg: ³cuz: ⁴bro, etc. ²<what's up __?>

doin dirt \ vb: doing illegal activities for pay or fun <some people have fun __>

D.O.G. *(acronym)* doing only gangster shit *(gang term)*

doggin \ vb: **dogged**: ¹to insult: ²to destroy ¹<he was __ his friend> ²<dogged his car>

doghouse \ n: ¹punishment from sex (ex. to sleep alone if an argument is not resolved): ²relationship troubles ¹<he was in the __ when he got caught lying to his girlfriend.>

dom \ ʻdäm \ n: a masculine lesbian <the __ loved her girlfriend>

don \ ʻdän \ n: ¹a person that hustles in a community and gives back: ²boss ¹<the __ in the city>

donkey \ ʻdän-kē \ n: ¹a female's butt: ²booty: ³ass: ⁴a turkey ¹<she's got a nice __>

donks \ ʻdōnks \ n: old cars with big rims <I like my car with __on it>

Donny Brasco \ n: ¹an undercover: ²C.I.: ³a snitch or rat ³<your cousin is a __ type of person>

¹dope \ 'dōp \ n: referring to drugs (ex. weed or coke) <the fiend buys a lot of __>

²dope \ adj: ¹nice or pleasant: ²a compliment: ³ill: ⁴great ¹<that song was __>

dope fiend \ -'fēn \ n: one who is addicted to drugs, usually crack or heroin

dork \ 'dȯrk \ n: a nerd or jerk or a lame <he's such a __>

doubling back \ vb: **doubled back**: to go back again: <the drug was so good that he doubled back>

dow \ 'daů \ n: ¹money: ²cheese: ³cake: ⁴bread, etc. ¹<to spend __>

¹down \ 'daůn \ adj: referring to someone being incarcerated <his brother's been __ for six years>

²down \ vb: ¹to conspire with someone to commit a crime: ²to engage in something, anything ¹<Rick was __ with the robbery>

³down \ adv: a sad emotion <Kate was feeling __ when her mom died>

downed \ 'daůn-ed \ vb: referring to someone getting murdered <the gang banger got __>

down packcd \ -'pak-ed \ vb: under control <everything is __>

drag net \ 'drag-'net \ adv: a set-up, usually involving multiple people <Tom's drug operation got caught in a __>

drawing \ 'drȯ-in \ vb: ¹drawing attention: ²tripping: ³buggin ²<the passenger started __ after waiting in line for over an hour>

¹dread \ 'drēd \ adj: nickname for a person of the Rastafarian religion or a person with dreads <the Jamaican __>

²dread \ adv: ¹great, heavy, hard or righteous wrath: ²serious times to a people or nation ²<Times are _.>

dripping \ adj: **drip**: ¹fresh: ²fly: ³confident ³<He was dripping with swagger __>

drop \ vb: **dropped**; **dropping the dime on** (··): ¹to injure or put pressure on a person: ²surprise: ³to kill ³<Rick was about to drop the dime on a friend that he thought was a snitch>

drop da ball \ vb: **dropping da ball**: ¹to lose: ²fall off ¹<I work real hard, so I don't drop da ball>

drought \ 'draůt \ adj: ¹a period when there are no drugs around or very little: ²a shortage of drugs ¹<when the __ came, he hiked up the prices for the drugs>

dry snitching \ 'drī-'snic-in \ vb: ¹indirectly giving out information knowingly or boldly giving out information jokingly: ²giving information without being asked ¹<Jake was __ when he jokingly told on his friend>

dub \ 'dəb \ n: ¹twenty dollars' worth of drugs: ²referring to the number twenty: ³twenty-inch rims ¹<he bought a __ worth of drugs> ³<car was setting on __>

duby \ 'dů-bē \ n: a small blunt or splif <he smoked a __>

duck \ 'dək \ adj: an unattractive woman <she's a __>

D.U.F.F *(acronym)* designated ugly fat friend

dump \ 'dəmp \ vb: to break up with someone that one is in a relationship with: dumped <Tom's girlfriend dumped him>

dumping \ 'dəmp-in \ vb: shooting <the police officers were __ at the suspect>

dunny boop \ ʻdün-ē-ˈbůp \ n: [1]two: [2]deuce [1]<two of something is considered a __>

early

.

early \ n: an expression of affirmation (ex. to exaggerate a statement) <I can't wait to go to my girlfriend's house __!>

ease dropping \ ʻez-ˈdräp-in \ vb: **eavesdropping**: to secretly listen to someone's conversation

eat \ ʻet \ vb: **eating**: to make money <everyone is trying to __>

eight ball \ ʻat-ˈbȯl \ n: 3.5 grams of cocaine

eighty-eight (88) \ ʻā-tē-ˈat \ n: [1]slang for police officers: [2]five-O [1]<the __ on the block>

egging on \ vb: to instigate or to force someone to do something

egg on your face \ adv: being embarrassed

elbow \ n: [1]life sentence: [2]L

err body \ ˌer-ˈbä-dē \ n: everybody

faded \ 'fād-ed \ vb: high or intoxicated <Jake was __ after a few smokes>

faggot \ 'fa-gət \ n: [1]a homosexual: [2]gay [1]<the proud __>

fallback \ 'föl-'bak \ vb: **falling back**; **fell back**: [1]staying out of commotion: [2]low key: [3]to chill [1]<he fell back for a while>

fart \ 'färt \ vb: **farted**: to pass gas <Tim farted in the crowd>

fassy \ 'fa-sə \ n: punk or lame person <the foolish __>

Fat shaming \ adj: to shame someone because they are overweight

Feeling you *(phrase)* to like someone, "I like you" <I'm __ >

feel me \ vb: phrase used when asking someone if they understand <you __?>

feisty \ 'fi-stē \ adj: to show emotional aggressiveness <the __ woman>

Felicia \ a female no one cares for

Fell off \ 'fel- \ vb: or **fallin off**: to lose once gained success or fame

Fell off the wagon *(phrase)* vb: or **fall off the wagon**: to relapse

fiend \ 'fēn \ n: a person that is addicted to drugs <the __ was addicted to crack>

financial freedom \ adj: unrestricted money resources available to a person

fire \ 'fīər \ adj: to compliment something or someone (ex. a song) <that song was __>

fish \ 'fēsh \ [1]n or [2]vb: **fishin**: [1]snitch: [2]looking for trouble [1]<Tim was a __> [2]<__ in for trouble>

fit·in·na \ 'fit-ē-na \ vb: *(contraction)* about to <I'm __ go to the mall>

five fifty \ 'fiv-fi-tē \ adv: *(code term)* [1]not in the circle anymore: [2]to alert the others in a gang that a snitch is around; *see bloods* [1]<a member of the gang was now a __>

Five O \ 'fiv-ō \ n: [1]the police: [2]the boys: [3]the pigs: [4]the fuzz [1]<the __ was arresting the robbers>

Five-star chick \ 'fīv-'stär-'chik \ adj: [1]a flawless woman: [2]a bad bitch: [3]a dime

Five Star General \ 'fīv-'stär-'je-nə- rəl \ adj: a boss or leader, usually involved in illegal activities <my dad is a __>

flag \ n: a bandana exhibiting a gang's color <waved his __>

[1]**flame** \ 'flām \ n: [1]a gun: [2]a burner: [3]a gat: [4]a heat [1]<he pulled out his __>

[2]**flame** \ adj: used as a compliment, same use as "fire" <that song was __>

flexing \ 'fleks-in \ vb: [1]showing off: [2]spending money: [3]showing off one's muscles [1]<after my bro won the lottery, he started to flex>

flip \ 'flip \ vb: **flipped**: [1]to double the amount of money initially invested in a particular project or to double the product, usually drugs: [2]to get mad at a person: [3]to kill someone [1]<he flipped his profits> [2]<Jeffrey flipped on his friend> [3]<flipped a man for money>

flipside \ - 'sīd \ n: the riverside of a story, usually the side that no one wants to hear <the __ of a story>

floss \ 'fläs \ vb: **flossing**: [1]to show off: [2]balling <rappers love to __>

flow \ 'flō \ vb: **flowing**: referring to one's own unique style or a musician's rhyming pattern <I like that rapper's flow>

fly \ 'flī \ adj: handsome, pretty, cute, awesome, or could be used as a compliment <a fly car or a fly girl>

flunky \ 'fləŋ-kē \ n: [1]one who serves or follow others to gain approval: [2]crash dummie or yes man [1]<the desperate __>

Folk Nation \ 'fōk-'nā-shən \ n: an urban gang

folks \ 'fōkz \ n: referring to a friend or family member <Tom's __ came to the party>

food \ 'füd \ n: [1]money, drugs or anything valuable: [2]target of violence [2]<Those boys over there are looking like __>

food chain \ - 'chān \ n: the flow of money and power on the streets

foodie \ n: a person that loves to cook and eat food

fool \ 'fül \ n: stupid, crazy or buffoon <Rick is a damn __>

[1]**fraud** \ 'fräd \ n: a person who frauds

[2]**fraud** \ vb: **frauding**: [1]to tell a lie: [2]to fake: [3]fugazy: [1]<Q frauding to his girl>

freak \ 'frēk \ adj: or **freaky**: a sexual person <the girl is a __>

Free balling \ 'frē-'bȯl-in \ vb: or **free ball**: [1]a male not wearing underwear: [2]going commando [1]<__ to work>

freeload \ 'frē-ˌlōd \ vb: or **freeloading**: to live off someone else <he __ off his mom>

fresh \ adj: [1]clean: [2]flirtatious behavior that is offensive due to age (ex. an underaged person flirting with an adult) [1]<he was __ when he got dressed > [2]<the 12-year old girl was being __ with an adult man>

from the gun buss *(phrase)*: [1]initially: [2]from the rip: [3]off the rip [1]<he was there from the __>

from the rip *(phrase)*: from the beginning <My mom was there _>

front \ 'frənt \ vb: **fronted** or **fronting**: [1]to give something on consignment: [2]to lend [1]<Ben fronted Tim some money>

frontin \ 'frənt-in \ vb: [1]to pretend: [2]to bluff: [3]not real with one's self or other: [4]to lie [1]<Ken always __ like he's rich>

fruit \ 'früt \ n: **fruity**: [1]a homosexual: [2]gay: [3]faggot [1]<"I think that boy is a __." said the thug.>

fruity \'frü-tē \ vb: to act feminine (ex. a male acting like a woman) <to act __>

F.S.U. *(acronym)*: friends stand united (gang term)

F·U·B·A·R *(acronym)*: f**ked up beyond all recognition

fugazy \ fü-gā-zē \ adj: [1]fake: [2]generic: [3]a fraud [1]<I'm not with the __ stuff>

fuzz \ 'fəz \ n: [1]the police: [2]five-o: [3]the boys: [4]the pigs [1]<the __ on the block>

G

.

[1]**G** \ 'G-ē \ n: gangsta

[2]**G's** \ n: stacks of one thousand <the G Spent G's in the club>

[1]**game** \ 'gām \ n: or **the game**: life style of illegal activities to make a living <he was rich in the __>

[2]**game** \ vb: or **to game** or **gaming** or **gave the game to**: [1]to trick someone: [2]being played or taken advantage of: [3]to give knowledge (as give you the game) [1]<KP was gaming his girl> [3]<the old head gave the game to the youngin>

gang \ 'gaŋ \ n: a group of like-minded persons <the __ started a riot>

Gang bang \ vb: **-banging; -banged**: [1]one woman having sex with many men at the same time [1]<the men gang banged a girl>: [2]to be raped

Gang banging \ vb: [1] living the gang life [1]<was __ to make money> [2]shooting at rival gangs

gangsta \ 'gan-stə \ n: [1]a real, smart, ruthless, confident, or ambitious person: *(a gangsta is not always a member of a gang): [2]dope: [3]thug: [4]gang leader [1]<the humble __> [2]<that car is __ . >

gank \ 'gank \ n: [1]good weed [1]<sold a lot of __>: [2]vb: to rob someone

gassed \ 'gas-ted \ vb: or **gassed up**: to instigate or influence or exaggerate a truth or lie <__ up his friend>

gat \ 'gat \ n: [1]a gun: [2]burner: [3]nina [1]<__s is bad>

G check \ 'G-'chek \ vb: [1]to give someone a reality check: [2]check or correct: [3]to test a gangsta's knowledge [1]<__ his brother> [3]<__a gang member>

G code \ 'G-ˈkōd \ n : ¹a G has to abide by the street code to be a G, says less, listens more, provides for family, one step ahead of the next best thing, being a trend setter, and or always an alpha male or female *(different hoods have different G-codes, but this is usually the moral conduct of the code.)* : ²abiding by the street code : ³a certain un-written rule that someone in the streets playing the game should follow

gear \ 'gir \ n: clothes, usually name brand designers <nice__>

¹geechy \ 'gē-chē \ adj: ¹amazing: ²to compliment: ³fly ¹<that dress is __!>

²geechy \ n: ¹referring to good weed: ²loud: ³exotic ¹<that wees is __!>

geek in \ 'gēk-in \ vb: ¹to brag about assets in a joking way: ²flossing: ³balling

generic \ 'de-ˈner-ik \ adj: ¹fake ²fugazy: ³a fraud ¹<I hate people with __ personalities>

get \ 'get \ vb: or **got** or **getting the drop on** (··); information or routine of a person being observed <the police got the drop on a drug dealer they were looking for>

get on the nipple *(phrase)*: go back to your mom: *(phrase used when calling a person, a momma's boy or girl)* <the girl told her boyfriend to __ while arguing.>

¹ghetto \ 'ge-tō \ n: ¹poor urban or suburban community: ²something that is broken ¹<the family is living in the __>

²ghetto \ adj: ¹one who is loud or disorderly in public: ²acting like a stereotyped black person: *vb:* ³coming from poverty: ⁴any race, baggy clothes and/or uneducated: ⁵something that needs to be fixed or replaced ¹<the girl acted __ in public > ³<living in the __> ⁴<the __ person>

ghetto youth \ n: poor kids or teens <the wise __>

ghost \ vb: or **ghosted**: ¹gone: ²to leave quickly: ³to kill someone ³<the man got __>

girling \ 'gərl-in \ adv: acting feminine <Tom was __ when he lost the bet>

G.K.B. *(acronym)* Gangsta Killa Blood, urban gang

glass \ 'glas \ n: meth and other amphetamines

goblin \ 'gä- bət \ n: ¹one with vulture like personality: ²higher ranking member than a goon or thug but under a gangsta ¹<the evil __>

godfather \ 'Gäd-ˌFa-thər \ n: ¹a retired drug king pin: ²a retired business man ²<the __ of the business >

go hard \ 'gō- \ vb: or **going hard**: ¹aggressive excellence: ²being the best one can be ²<the rapper was going hard in the studio>: ³going whole hog

going dutch *(phrase)*: ¹splitting the bill on a date: ²Dutch ¹<after a bad first date, Tom asked his date if they were __>

going whole hog \ vb: ¹going to the extreme: *(syn)* ²goin hard ¹<the man was __ in the contest>

going against the grain \ vb: ¹to go against the odds: ²going against one's morals: ³disagreement: ⁴opposite

gold digger \ 'gōld-'dēg-er \ n: ¹a person who uses charm or trickery to get money, gifts, or property from others, usually a female gold digging a man: *vb*: [2]using charm or trickery to get what one wants [1]<the tricky __>

good looking \ 'gǔd-'lǔk-in \ n: thank you <__ for lending me that money>

[1]**good money** \ adj: or [2]**bad money**: [1]trust worthy or OK to work with: [2]not trust worth or OK to work with

goon \ 'gün \ n: [1]a disruptive, disrespectful person or a ruthless and not so smart person: [2]thug [1]<the ruthless __>

gossip queen\n: or **gossip king**: a person who habitually reveals personal facts or a person who spreads rumors

got got \ 'gät-gät \ vb: to be robbed or cheated out of something <Tim __ for his smart phone>

got heart \ 'gät-'härt \ adj: referring to a person that is brave or is being brave <little Billy __ for standing up to the bully>

Government name \ n: the name one's parent gave them legally and on one's birth certificate <he used his __ on the job application>

G.P. *(acronym)* general purpose

G raised \ g-'rāz \ n: grandmother raised *(used in the Pittsburgh area)* <my older brother was G raised when our dad left>

gravy \ 'grāvē \ adj: [1]cool: [2]chill: [3]okay or all right [1]<everything __>

green \ 'grēn \ n: weed <smoked some strong __>

grenade \ grə-'nād \ adj: an ugly companion of a pretty female <out of the three girls <I got the __ out of the group>

grill \ 'gril \ n: or **grillz**: [1]decorative tooth veneers or caps: [2]teeth <the boy had really nice grillz>

grill in \ 'gril-iŋ \ vb: to boldly look in a person's face, or to look at a person in general <my ex was __ my new girl>

grimy \ 'grīmē \ adj: [1]untrustworthy person or a shady situation: [2]disloyal, sneaky, or tricky: [3]a bad situation [2]<the __ business man>

grind \ 'grīnd \ n: [1]a job or skill [1]<everyone needs a __> vb: [2]to work hard

grinding \ 'grīnd-iŋ \ vb: [1]working hard at a task: [2]hustling: [3]selling drugs or making money [1]<mom was __ hard to make ends meet>

grinding up \ 'grīnd-iŋ-əp \ vb: grind up: [1]to make fun of someone or to embar-rass them: [2]to buss on <Rick was __ his brother because he had a booger on his face>

groupie \ 'grüpē \ n: a person that will do anything to get close to a super star <the __ was willing to do anything for some tickets>

grub \ 'grəb \ vb: or **grubbing**: [1]to eat food: [2]referring to food [1]<grubbing on a steak>

G stance \ 'g-'stans \ n: referring to a gangsta's posture or how he stands or poses with swag <the gangsta privately worked on his __>

G stroll \ -'strōl \ n or vb: a slow walk intending to impress others: **G strolled** <Pete g-strolled down the block full of girls>

gucci \'guchē \ n: good, cool, relaxed, or satisfied <I'm feeling __>

gunning \'gən-iŋ \ vb: [1]speeding: [2]aggressive sexual intercourse [1]<the car was __ down the highway> [2]<the man was __ his wife in bed>

gwap \ ghäp \ n: [1]money: [2]cheese: [3]bread: [4]cake: [5]mula: [6]dow [1]<spent his__>

half \ 'haf \ n: half ounce of weed or half pound, usually referring to weed but can be referring to other drugs

H·A·M *(acronym)* hard as a mother f**ker

[1]**hammer** \ 'ha-mər \ n: [1]a pistol or gun: [2]referring to a penis [1]<the police officer used his __> [2]<the girl sucked on his __>

[2]**hammered** \ 'ha-mər-ed \ vb: referring to one being high or drunk <the man was __>

hamming it up \ vb: over playing something <the artist was __ so the crowd would get hyped>

hard \ n: [1]crack cocaine: [2]ready rock: [3]a man being horny[1]<sold some __ to a fiend>

hashtag \ 'hash-tag \ n: a number sign followed by the subject of one's internet posting, trending online <#theuniversalslangdictionary>

hater \ 'hāt-er \ n: a person who dislikes another's progress, usually for no apparent reason <the broke __>

hating \ 'hāt-iŋ \ vb: [1]disliking progress or something good for no apparent reason: [2]trying to stop progress for no apparent reason: [3]throwing shade[1]<the police officer was __ on the inmate's release>

Have an axe to grind *(phrase):* [1]something to complain about: [2]selfish reason for doing something; [3]ulterior motive <Jim had an __ with his man>

hawk \ 'hȯk \ vb: or **hawked**: to chase something or someone down <the lady hawked down the bus so she would not miss it>

haze \ hāz \ vb: or **hazing**: to harass by abusive and humiliating tricks, usually forcing someone to drink until they vomit

head \ 'hed \ n: [1]oral sex: [2]brain: [3]top: [4]chopper [1]<he enjoys getting __>

head hunting \ -'hənt-in \ vb: searching for a victim, most often to kill them <the gang was __ for their enemy>

headz up \ adv: [1]to give warning to: [2]to stay focused [1]<gave the man __ on the oncoming car>

heat \ 'hēt \ n: [1]fire arm: [2]hot [1]<the man was packing __> vb: [3]being investigated by the police[3]<drawing __>

Hells Angels \ 'helz - \ n: biker gang originating in Ohio

hemmed up \ 'hem-ed-əp \ vb: to get caught or stuck in a place or situation <they got __ in the crowd>

hick \ hik \ n: [1]a white person usually from the countryside, can also be used as a derogatory term: [2]cracker: [3]red neck

high \ 'hī \ vb: [1]intoxicated on drugs or alcohol: [2]faded [1]<__ on drugs>

hill Billy \ 'hil-billē \ n: [1]white person from the country; can also be used as a derogatory term: [2]hick

hill toe \ n: the name of a dance

[1]**hit** \ 'hit \ vb: [1]to have sexual intercourse: [2]bang: [3]smash: [4] to inhale smoke from doing a drug or to inject with a needle, usually used by drug addicts: [5]referring to someone getting shot [1]<Pablo asked his friend if he __ the girl he met last night> [4]<the fiend gave his buddy a __ of coke> [5]<Tate got __ up last night by the police officers>

[2]**hit** \ adj: [1]an unattractive person: [2]single dose of a drug [1]<that chick is __> [2]<can I get a __>

hit a lick \ vb; or **buss a lick**: [1]to rob someone: [2]to sell drugs [1]<Ronny was down to __>

ho \ 'hō \ n: [1]a promiscuous female: [2]a term used to refer to any female in general in conversation amongst friends: [3]hooker [1]<the tricky __>

holla \ 'hä-la \ vb: [1]to have a conversation with a person: [2]concluding remarks at parting (ex. good bye) [1]<let me __ at you real quick>

holla-back \ adv: talk to you later or come again <I'll __ at you later>

homie \ 'hōmē \ n: [1]a friend: [2]cuz, B, bro, or son, etc. [2]<what's up __>

Hoochie momma \ 'hŭ-chē-'mä-mä \ n: a ghetto girl who wears little or tight clothes to show off her curves <your baby's mother dresses like a __>

hood \ 'hŭd \ n: [1]an urban community: [2]the streets: [3]the ghetto <the police officers are always in the __>; the hood

hood nigga \ n: a person from the hood who knows the G code and street code and plays the game

hookup \ 'hŭk- \ vb: [1]to sell stolen goods for cheap: [2]to give someone a good deal: [3]to get together with: [4]to have sex with [4]<they hooked up last night>

hoopty \ n: [1]an old car: [2]a car that needs fixing [1]<was driving a __>

[1]**hot** \ 'hät\ vb: [1]unwanted attention by the police officers or robbers brought upon a person involved in illegal activities: [2]involved in illegal activities: [3]heat [1]<the block is __>:

[2]**hot** \ n: [1]to compliment excellence or beauty: [2]on fleek: [3]fire: [4]flame [2]<that track was __>

house mouse \ n: a maid or housewife of a gang member <the __ was living in fear>

House in Virginia *(acronym)* HIVs.

house nigga \ n: [1]a African American who snitches on someone of his own race to help the police or authorities: [2]a snitching inmate: [3]a African American who helps white people more than his own [1]<J is such a __>

hum bug \ 'həm- \ vb: hearing something by coincidence or out of the blue

hurled \ 'hərl-ed \ vb: to overpower <the man __ his son in a play fight?

husla \ 'hə-sela \ n: [1]a business man: [2]one who is constantly trying to make money [2]<the sharp__>

hush money \ n: [1]money given to someone for them to keep a secret or keep silent: [2]blackmail [1]<he gave his ex __ to not tell his wife that he cheated on her>

hype \ 'hīp \ vb: [1]showing off: [2]to act cocky: [3]amped <I was __ after I won the lottery>

.

I bang wit you *(phrase)* [1]I get along with you: [2]to engage in a violent act with a person, usually a gang member

ice \ 'is \ n: [1]jewelry, usually gold, silver, platinum, or diamond: [2]meth and fedimy [1]<wears a lot of __> [2]<got buzzed with __>

iced \ 'is-ed \ vb: [1]referring to a person being killed: [2]hit up <got __>

iced out \ 'ised_ \ adj: describing a person with a lot of jewelry on

I.d.k. *(acronym)* I don't know

I got you *(phrase)* a phrase used when telling someone that they are protected or well taken care of <don't worry __>

ill \ 'il \ adj: [1]the best person, place or thing: [2]thorouel: [3]real: [4]dope: [6]nice [6]<that song is _>

Illest \ 'il-est \ adj: the best of the best person, place or thing <that's the __ thing I ever seen>

In da cut \ 'in-da-'kət \ adj: a secret location or referring to being low key <the boss lives __>

In da loop \ 'in-da-'lŭp \ vb: being up to date with the latest trends <my little brother stays __>

In da way \ 'in-da-'wā \ adv: [1]blocking the progress of people including one's self: [2]one doing too much [1]<senseless killers are __>

informer \ 'in-'for-mər \ n: [1]snitch: [2]rat: [3]stool pigeon [1]<the __ was shot after court>

inked \iŋk-ed \ vb: referring to being tattooed <the ball player was being __>

In (··) bag \ vb: going hard, focused, or confident *(replace (··) with proper pronoun)* <Jay was really in his bag at the game>

Insta violence \ ˌin-stə-ˈvī-ləns \ vb: video or picture of violence being posted on Instagram <people should stop the __>

In the buff *(phrase)* naked

In the mix \ vb: [1]involved in illegal activities: [2]caught up: [3]in the midst of creating something

---

jacked \ vb: [1]to punch or attack someone: [2]to steal: [3]to get excited [1]<he got __> [2]<__the car> [3]<Steve was __ when he won some money>

jack boys \ ʻjak-ˈbȯi \ n: robbers <the __ robbed the bank>

jacket \ ʻja-kət \ n: [1]prison record or criminal history: [2]rap sheet <has a long __>

jack-of-all-trades \ n: [1]a person that is good at all trades or has a basic knowledge of a lot of trades: [2]professional [1]<her husband is the __>

jack off \ vb [1]to masturbate: [2]cash a check: [3]stealing; jacking off [1]<was jacking off to porno>

[1]**jakes** \ ʻjāks \ n: [1]the police: [2]five-o: [3]the boys [1]<the __ shot a man>

[2]**Jake** *(contraction)* Jamaican

jam \ ʻjam \ vb: a stick up or robbery; or **jammed** <they got jammed at the park>

jawn \ ʻjȯn \ n: [1]girl or woman: [2]bitch: [3]biddie: [4]anything physical or abstract [1]<that __ pretty> [4]<that __ in the sky>

jay \ ʻjā \ n: or **jayied**: [1]a marijuana cigarette: [2]to get high off drugs [1]<they smoked a __>

J'z \ ʻjāz \ n: nick name for "Jordens", basketball player Michael Jorden's sneakers <was wearing custom made __>

jet \ ʻjet \ vb: jetted: [1]to run quickly: [2]ghosted [1]<jetted to the bus stop>

jew \ 'jü \ adj: a person that's tight with money <Joe was called a __ because he was stingy>

jip \ 'jēp \ vb: a commonly used misspelling of "gyp" which means to steal or cheat

joe \ 'jō \ adj: [1]to be overly lame: [2]corny [1]<the __ girl>

Joe familiar \ - 'fə-'mil-yər \ n: a person that is too friendly with strangers <mother warned her son about being a __>

[1]**joint** \ n: [1]blunt or splif: [2]weed rolled and ready to smoke [1]<smoked a __>

[2]**joint** \ n: or **The Joint**: [1]referring to jail or prison: [2]anything physical or abstract [1]<Kim went to the __>

jones in \ 'jōnz-in \ vb: craving or fiening for something <Jake was __ for some more drugs>

jonny \ 'jä-nē \ n: [1]a stolen car: [2]referring to a penis: [3]manns: [4]dick: [5]pipe

juice\adj: or **I got the juice**: [1]swagger: [2]sauce or saucy

[1]<my girlfriend got da juice>

jump \ 'jəmp \ vb: [1]two or more persons fighting one person: [2]a gang versus one person: [3]to outnumber one in a fight: jumped [1]<Billy got jumped by four people>

jump-off \ n: [1]a side chick: [2]promiscuous woman: [3]a booty call [1]<he called his __ after he broke up with his girl>

Justin Bieber \ n: [1]referring to coke or cocaine: [2]white girl: [3]Miley Cyrus [1]<the dealer was selling __>

jux \ 'jəkz \ vb: to rob someone or referring to a robbery <Chris got jux for his chain>

keep it a bean

.

keep it a bean \ vb: or **keeping it a bean** or **kept it a bean**: [1]truthful: [2]keeping it 100%: **keeping it 100%** \ vb: [1]to tell the full truth: [2]keeping it a bean: [3]keeping it real: **keep it real** \ vb: [1]to be honest: [2]keeping it 100%: [3]keeping it a bean

ketamine \ 'ket-a-min \ n: street drugs containing horse and cat tranquilizer

key \ 'kē \ n: [1]kilo, used to refer to drug quantity: [2]referring to success

k·hole \ 'k-ole \ vb: a zone or high like state stemming from the use of street drug ketamine

kick back \ 'kik_ \ vb: to chill or relax

kicks \ 'kikz \ n: sneakers

killa \ 'killa \ n: [1]referring to a friend as bro, cuz, etc. [1]<what's up __>: [2]weed

killing it \ 'kil-in-ət \ vb: [1]something done perfectly: [2]going hard: [3]brilliant: [4]murda

kill Zac \ 'kil-zak \ n or adv: referring to anyone or to get someone's attention nearby, mainly used by the Bloods <Yo __!>

kinfo \ 'kin-fō \ n: friend or family <the guy hugged his __>

knocked up \ 'näk-ed - \ vb: a woman being pregnant

knockers \ 'nä-kərz \ n: [1]a women's breasts: [2]tities <size D __>

knock me \ 'nark- \ vibe: [1]referring to one getting hurt or sabotaged by somebody else or played: [2]to be tricked [1]<haters trying to __>

knock off \ vb: or **knocked off**: to murder or kill someone or to finish or empty something <the young man got knocked off> <the hungry man knocked off his plate of food> n: ¹something fake: ²generic ¹<he had a __ Gucci belt>

L

.

<u>**loc'd in**</u>   **L**

L \ 'el \ n: ¹blunt or joint of weed ¹<smoked a __> vb: ²to lose or fall ²<took a __>: ³fall from grace

ladder \ 'la-dər \ n: an extended clip for a gun

laid an egg \ vb: referring to a show that flopped

lame \ 'lām \ vb: boring or wack

lango \ 'laŋ-gō \ n: slang, secret language used to communicate amongst gang members

latch \ 'lach \ vb: to get married

lick \ 'lik \ vb: or **bussed a lick**: ¹to make easy money, usually illegally: ²robbery ¹<they bussed a __>

lil buddy \ 'li-- \ n: female friend or girlfriend

lil nigga \ 'li -- \ n: small timer, low ranking person

lit \ 'lit \ vb: ¹high or faded or intoxicated: ²wiz: ³flashy ¹<they got so __ on the weed>

lip service \ vb: talkative

L·M·A·O *(acronym)* laughing my ass off

loc'd in \'läk·ed- \ vb: initiated into something, usually a gang <they told the new gang member that he was __>

lofted \ ‘lȯft-ed \ vb: high, lit, or faded, etc. <they were __ on the weed>

Logan Heights \ n: Hispanic gang

L.O.L. *(acronym)* laughing out loud

looking for the business \ vb: [1]flirting: [2]look for work [1]<she was __ with a handsome guy>

loosies \ ‘lüs-es \ n: or **lucies** or **lucys**: loose cigarettes, usually sold individually

loud \ ‘laůd \ n: exotic weed, usually high dro <they smoked __>

love boat \ ləv-- \ n: weed dipped in P.C.P. weed mixed with wet <they were smoking a __>

lovies \ ‘ləv-ēz \ n: bags of weed <the dealer had some __ in his pocket>

loving the crew \ vb: referring to a promiscuous female, sexually involved with multiple persons from the same crew <the girl had sex with all three brothers, she’s __>

low-key \ vb: [1]being successful without drawing attention: [2]under the radar <the rich guy kept real __>: [3]engaged in a criminal lifestyle, but not on the police radar

lunching \ ‘lənch-iŋ \ vb: not paying attention in general or being lazy or slacking <the guy was __ on his enemies so he got killed>

mack \ 'mak \ n: [1]a person who speaks with seductiveness or persuasion to get what he/she wants: [2]pimp [1]<the smooth __>

macking \ vb: [1]seductive or persuasive talk to get what one wants: [2]pimping: [3]mack [1]<the player was __ to his girl>

[1]made \ 'mād \ n: to attain the highest level in a criminal organization <I'm a __man>

[2]made \ vb: to be discovered by the law or robbers <the dealer was __ by the cops>

ma fault \ 'mī-'fòlt \ adj: [1]an apology, usually "sorry": [2]my bad

main man \ 'mān \ n: speaking of someone in general <__ is coming to court>

manz \ 'manz \ n: or **manns**: [1]a friend: [2]peeps [1]<dats my __>: [3] referring to a "penis" [3]<the fool got arrested for pulling his __ out in public>

Marley \ mär-lē \ n: [1]weed: [2]mary jane: [3]gank: [4]bud <they smoked some __>

Mary Jane \ 'mārē-'jān \ n: [1]weed: [2]marley: [3]gank <they smoked some __>

math \ 'math \ n: phone number

mean mug \ n: or **mean mugging**: a mean or unfriendly facial expression

merk \ 'mərk \ vb: [1]to kill: [2]merked: [3]x'd out: [4]to knock off <people in the hood get merked every day>

M·I·A *(acronym)* missing in action

.

Miley Cyrus \ n: [1]pills usually *Molly*: [2]Justin Bieber [1]<he popped a __>

mit \ 'mēt \ n: hand <the guy put gloves on his __>

miz \ 'mi-z \ n: mom or mother

mo \ 'mō \ n: [1]cuz, bro, nigga, etc. *(used in D.C.) adj*: [2]more

M.O.B *(acronym)* [1]money over bitches: [2]business over pleasure

M·O·F·O *(acronym)* mother f**ker

molly \'mäl·ē \ n: [1]extasy pills: [2]Miley Cyrus

money on deck \ adj: money on hand

money on wood \ adj: money on hand during a bet: [2]good money [1]<Jim got his __>

money pit \ n: something that requires a lot of money or something that is taking money away from a person <this old house is a __>

monkey \ 'məŋ-kē \ n: [1]referring to a *"female's butt"*: [2]donkey: [3]ass: [4]booty, etc. [1]<she has a nice __>: [5]AIDS or HIV [5]<Kate tested positive for the __>

monsta \ 'män-stā \ n: [1]a person who will not accept or be content with anything less than perfection: [2]a person who goes hard on whatever they do [1]<he is a __ at everything>

mo \ 'mō \ adj: more <__money, __ problems>

mop \ 'mäp \ adj: unskilled loser <Larry is a __ at softball>

mugga \ 'muga \ n: [1]money: [2]cake: [3]cheese: [4]mula [1]<banks put their __ in a safe>

mula \ n: [1]money: [2]mugga: [3]cake: [4]bread: [5]cheese, etc. <spent his __ on a car>

murda \ 'mərda \ adj: [1]brilliant or nice: [2]murder [1]<the artist murdered that track>

my bad \ adj: [1]sorry: [2]my fault [1]<__ for spilling that drink on your new shirt>

nabbed

.

nabbed \ 'nab-ed \ vb: or **nab**: [1]kidnapped: [2]snatched up <the little girl got __ last night>

nagget \ 'nag-ət \ n: a piece of information <I got some __ for you>

naw \ 'nā \ adv: no <you going to the club? __>

neutrals \ 'nŭ-trəl-z \ n: non-gang members

nice \ adj: [1]a compliment: [2]sick <Dan's rim on that car is __>

nickel \ 'ni-kəl \ n: five dollars-worth of drugs or referring to the number five in general

nigga \ 'nīg-a \ n: [1]common term used amongst friends, usually referring to a person [1]<what's up with dem niggas>: [2]an ignorant person: *or **niggas***

niggaritest \ 'nig-ga-rit-est \ n: or **da itest**: a state of tiredness or laziness after eating *(used by African Americas)* <Jim got __ after his Thanksgiving dinner>

nil zaw \ 'nēl-zå \ adv: [1]no: [2]naw [1]<the boy asked his dad if he could go outside, but his father said "__">

nina \ 'nēna \ n: [1]a 9mm hand gun: [2]heat: [3]a strap: [4]a gat: [5]burner [1]<most police officers carry ninas>

nit-picking \ 'nit -- \ vb: starting petty arguments or complaining about petty issues with a person <the police officer was __ with a suspect>

no doubt \ nō - \ adv: [1]yes or OK: [2]word up [1]<you like money? __>

no homo \ adj: not gay or homosexual, usually used after a sentence that would be perceived as a gay statement <that nigga got nice teeth __>

no puns intended *(phrase):* no disrespect to you *(ex. used when an irony statement has been made)* <__, but I don't like your mom>

No RIP *(acronym)* no reckless internet posting

no sauce \ vb: [1]not wanting any problems or competition: [2]no smoke: [3]no shade [1]<those niggas don't want no sauce>

no smoke \ adv: no sauce <dem boyz don't want __>

notted \ 'nät-təd \ vb: being in a deep sleep <he was __>

nut \ n: [1]semen: [2]cum [1]<bussed a __ in his girl> adj: [3]a crazy person

nutty \ adj: [1]something unbelievable or a stupid hostile situation: [2]trippin <a __ situation>3crazy

ock \ ək \ n: referring to a person *(ex. as a son, cuz, bro, etc.)* <what's up __?>

official \ 'ə-ˈfi-shə \ adj: [1]one who is legit: [2]a safe or good business deal <the deal is __>

off the chain *(phrase)* vb: [1]fun: [2]wild: *(syn)* [3]exciting: *(adj)* [4]not regular [1]<the party was __>

off the rip \ vb: [1]first: [2]from the gun buss [1]<he got the new iPhone __>

[1]**O. G** \ 'O-G \ n: [1]original gangsta: [2]gang leader: [3]a boss: [4]older guy

[2]**O. G** \ adj: someone who overcame a hardship and is now experienced and skilled in it <she's now an __ at acting>

O·G Status \ adj: boss status <my brother is __ at his new job>

old lady \ 'ōld_ \ n: a girlfriend <I love my __>

O·M·G *(acronym)* O My God

on \ vb: [1]connected: [2]successful: [3]intoxicated or high [2]<Ray just bought a new car, he must be __> [3]<Ray had too many drinks, he's __ right now>

on deck \ adj: [1]having something on hand: [2]ready: [3]money on wood [2]<have your money __ when I come>

one-time \ n: [1]the police: [2]five-o: [3]the fuzz: [4]the boys: [5]the pigs [1]<The__ outside arresting Mick>

onion \ n: [1]a women's butt: [2]ass: [3]booty: [4]cake

on fleek \ 'än-flēk \ adj: [1]something likeable: [2]hot: [3]flame: [4]fire <my car is __>

on (··) top \ vb: [1]to annoy someone or to become a nuisance to someone: [2]to pursue a person, usually for unpaid debt [1]<Rick was on his top for his unpaid debt>*(replace underscore with a possessive noun or pronoun, my, her, their, etc.)*

on one \ vb: [1]high on drugs: [2]lit: [3]wiz: [4]drunk: [5]wasted [1]<Jeff is __>

[1]**on point** \ vb: [1]focused: [2]ready: [3]aware: [4]the right amount [1]<stay _>

[2]**on point** \ adj: [1]to compliment something *(ex. a car)*: [2]nice: [3]hott <the food is __>

on site \ vb: to physically handle an altercation wherever one may be <when he saw the guy that hit his sister, it was __?>

on the fence \ adv: unsure or undecided

on the wagon \ vb: [1]being drunk: [2]wasted under the influence of drugs [1]<my mom was __ after two drinks>

on trend \ adj: something currently popular in the news or online or society <the new iPhone is __>

out chea \ 'aůt-chir \ adj: out here <we __ waiting on you> out here

outta pocket \ 'aůt-ta-'pä-kət \ adj: [1]disrespectful or out of line: [2]stingy [1]<the girl was __ when she spit on her boyfriend>

over the top \ vb: [1]taking something to the extreme: [2]going ham [1]<the artist went __ with his performance>

pad \ 'pad \ n: [1]a house: [2]a crib: [3]a spot [1]<had a nice __>

packed \ 'pak-əd \ adj: a crowded area <the club was __>

Pagans \ 'pā-gəz \ n: biker gang

panties in a bunch *(phrase)*: [1]up tight or confused: [2]people in a state of confusion or chaos: [3]scared [2]<They had their _ when the hurricane hit unexpectedly.>

parlaying \ 'pär-͵lā-iŋ \ vb: or **parlay** or **parlayed**: relaxing <after work he parlayed>

partied\vb: multiple people having sex with the same person *(usu. a female being partied.)* <_ the drunk girl.>

paypa \ 'pā-pa \ n: [1]money: [2]dow: [3]cheese: [4]gwap: [5]bread [1]<save his __>

Peace out \ n: good bye: [2]deuces [1]<__yo>

pearl \ vb: to leave <I'm about to __ outta here>

Peeling his wig \ vb: or **peeled his wig**: [1]taking someone's head off: [2]to shoot in the head [1]<the police officer peeled his wig>

Peep da blitz \ vb: or **peep da bliss**: [1]to pay attention to a particular event: [2]on point [1]<yo, __ they are about to fight>

Peep game \ 'pēp_ \ vb: [1]check this out [1]<yo! __>: [2]to put one's attention on a particular thing

Pee wee \ pē͵wē \ n: young gang member: *(see zoe pound)* <the new __>

pen \ n: [1]jail: [2]slammer

peps \ 'pēpz \ n: friend or family member

perkalator \ ʻpərk-a-lā-tor \ n: a type of dance

perks \ n: Percocet

pet name \ n: affectionate or passionate nick name

phat \ ʻfat \ adj: [1]something very likeable: [2]da boom: [3]banging: [4]fly: [5]on fleek

Phat ass \ adj: sexy big butt

PhD *(acronym)* punking head deluxe or a swollen face or playa hater degree

Photo bombing \ ʻfō-tō-ʻbäm=in \ vb: interrupting a photo shoot by jumping in unexpectedly

piece \ ʻpēs \ n: [1]a gun: [2]girl: [3]chain or pendant

pigs \ n: the police

pillow talk\vb: or **pillow talked** or **pillow talking**: laying in the bed or talking on the phone with your significant other, talking about other people's business or revealing secrets. <I never tell my friend my business because he always pillows talk with his girlfriend>

pimp \ n: [1]a person that makes his or her money from prostitutes: [2]a male or female that has more than one partner: [3]a mack

pimping \ vb: [1]macking: [2]making money from prostitutes: [3]having multiple partners at the same time

pinched \ ʻpinch-ed \ vb: arrested

pinner \ ʻpin-əd \ n: a small blunt or joint or splif <smoked the last of his __>

pipe \ n: penis

pipe up\vb: or **piped up** or **piping up**: to instigate by way of flattery

<Piped up his friend to do his work, by telling him he was really smart.>

playa \ 'plāə \ n: [1]mack: [2]pimp: [3]hustla: [4]drug dealer: [5]anybody that is getting money and in the mix: [6]a person who has multiple partners: [7]a customer, usually a drug dealer, referring to one of his customers as one of his "playas": [8]fien

played \ vb: [1]to be cheated on or cheated out of something or to be embarrassed: [2]lose: [3]fail [1]<Kate got __ by her boyfriend>

plug \ n: [1]a supplier or connect of drugs: [2]distributor of drugs [1]<the big homey has a good __>

P.M. *(acronym)* personal message

point \ n: an eighth of a kilo

poke \ vb: to stab; **-poked**

pop or **popped** \ vb: [1]to shoot someone: [2]to have sex with: [3]died [3]<someone got popped last night>

pop dat \ vb: referring to having sex: **popped dat** <he __ last night>

pop off \ vb: or **popped off** or **popping off**; [1]the beginning of controversy: [2]engaging in a fight: [3]verbally abusive [1]<things about to pop off> [2]<the fight popped off> [3]<the angry customer started popping off his mouth to the cashier for short changing him>

popo \ 'pō-pō \ n: [1]police: [2]five-o: [3]pigs: [4]one time

poppie \ pope \ n: or **Papie** or **Papi**: [1]Mexican or Hispanic nature: [2]referring to a person: *(syn)* [3]nigga [2]<what's up __?>

poppin \ adj: ¹good or exciting: ²hott: ³fun ¹<the party was __ last night>

Poppin tags \ vb: spending a lot of money; **-pop tags** <they closed the mall for my friend because he was guaranteed to pop tags>

Pop the five \ n: secret hand shake, *(the respect of the five-point star see "Bloods")*

pot head \ n: a person that is addicted to weed

¹**pound** \ n: ¹a fist bump: ²16 ounces of marijuana ¹<gave him a __ on the way out> ²<bought a __ from the dealer>

²**pound** \ vb: ¹to pound: ²to have sex: ³smash: ⁴hit: ⁵pop dat: -**pounding** ²<she liked how he was pounding her>

pree \ 'prē \ vb *(Jamaican Slang)*: to watch or observe; **-preeied** <the police officer preeied the robber before arresting him>

pressing \ vb: ¹to sweat someone: ²to consistently pressure a person or an issue: ³aggrevating ²<__ his mom for money

probie \ prōb-ē \ n: ¹new recruit in a gang: ²prospect <the unexperienced __>

prospect \ 'prä-ˌspekt \ n: ¹member in the training stages of a gang (see Breeds): ²probie <the new __>

P's and Q's \ vb: ¹being attentive and staying focused: ²on point

Pump faking \ adv: frauding or lying

punked \ vb: ¹to be pranked: ²chumped: ³bullied

puppy love\n: an immature or high intense feeling of love towards a person that is usually short lived <The young couple was in __>

pushed out the whip \ vb: no longer a part of the set or gang <Q got __ for snitching>

pushing\vb: selling drugs <Mike was _ weight.>

Put in work \ vb: [1]doing criminal acts: [2]working hard: [3]grinding: [4]buss a lick <the gang __ on that robbery last night> putting in work

putt \ vb: [1]knocked out: [2]killed or unconscious [2]<J got __ yesterday>

QP

.

quicky   Q

Q·P *(acronym)* quater pound of weed

quater \ n: referring to the number 25 or $25 worth of drugs

quicky \ 'kwik-ē \ vb: sex in a hurry

racks \ 'rakz \ n: [1]stacks of a thousand dollars [1]<he brought __ to the club>: [2]a woman's breasts [2]<she had size D __>

racket \ 'ra-kət \ n: another term for a fire arm <the thug fired his __>

raid \ 'rād \ vb: invasion, usually by the police into a person's house; raided <the drug dealer's house got raided>

[1]**rap** \ 'rap \ n: a conversation or a rhyme; rapping; rapped <the guy rapped to his girl>

[2]**rap** \ vb: or **no rap**: to end a conversation abruptly <I have no rap for you>

rap sheet \ n: criminal history <the felon had a long __>

Rasta \ 'ras-ta \ n: [1]Rastafarian religion from the Ethiopian orthodox church: [2]referring to a person who practices Rastafarian

rat \ 'rat \ n: [1]snitch: [2]stoll pigeon: [3]informant [1]<the __ testified on his friend>

ratchet \ 'ra-chət \ adj: [1]a ghetto person: [2]one who has a nasty attitude mentally or disorderly in behavior: [3]a gun [1]<the __ people>; adv: [4]not right

ratting \ vb: [1]to snitch: [2]to rat: [3]to tell <was __ on his brother>

rave \ 'rāv \ n: a party with a lot of drugs and music <the __ was crowded>

ready rock \ n: [1]crack cocaine: [2]hard: [3]rocks [1]<smoked __>

real \ 'rēl \ adj: [1]smart: [2]authentic: [3]original: [4]truthful [4]<he kept it __ with the judge>

realest \ adv: being the best and most truthful in a thing <Lil Wayne is the __ rapper>

real nigga \ n: a real person <my big bro is a __>

real one\n: [1]an original person who is truthful and smart: [2]real nigga: [3]thoroughbred

real rap \ adj: [1]honestly: [2]real talk [1]<what he spoke was __>

real shit \ adj: [1]to affirm to someone that you are telling the truth: [2]to question the truth: [3]a serious situation [1]<I won the lottery, __> [2]<__, did he really win?> [3]<this is some __ we're in>

real talk \ adj: [1]truthfully speaking: [2]real rap: [3]honestly [1]<I won the lottery, __>

[1]**rebound** \ ˌrē-baůnd \ adj: [1]a person that replaces an ex after a break up, usually right after a break up: [2]side chick [1]<she was his __>

[2]**rebound** \ vb: or **rebounded** or **rebounding**: [1]to get back in the dating pool after a break up: [2]getting back in a relationship after a break up [1]<It took Jake a while to __>

rebound sex \ vb: [1]to have sex with a new partner after a break up: [2]to have sex with a former partner [1]<they enjoyed their __>

[1]**reck** \ vb: or **recked** or **recking**: to crash or destroy <Kate recked her car>

[2]**reck** \ adj: ugly, ashy or unattractive <she is a __>

red bone \ n: a light skinned chick/woman <the pretty __>

red-neck \ n: Caucasian usually from the south or from the countryside

redrags \ n: Blood gang member

reefa \ 'rē-fa \ n: [1]weed: [2]tree: [3]green: [4]marley: [5]marijuana: [6]pot, etc. <got high off __>

re-up \ 're- \ vb: to buy more product, usually drugs; **re-ed up** <doubled his money on the re up>

[1]ride \ 'rīd \ n: car <wash and waxed his __>

[2]ride \ vb: to accompany a person <let's __>

rider \ 'rī-dər \ n: a person that remains loyal and takes risks for another person even through rough situations <Rayon is a __>

rider chick \ n: a woman who takes risk and remains loyal to her boyfriend or husband even through rough situations <Samantha is a __>

riding dirty \ vb: to transport illegal products usually drug or guns <Ken was __ all the way to New York>

riff raff \ 'rif-ˌraf \ vb: commotion or confusion <his friend loved to be in the __>

RIP *(acronym)* rest in peace

rip on \ 'rip-ȯn \ vb: or **ripped on** or **ripping on**: [1]to make fun of someone: [2]buss on <ripped on his friend>

ripped \ adj: muscular <that guy is __>

rips \ vb: drug robberies <the rivalry gang went on a series of __>

riz \ n: parents <every kid needs their __>

robbery \ vb: referring to stealing a friend's girlfriend or a girl that a friend was attempting to date

rock \ vb: or **rocked**: referring to a knock out or one being knocked out <that guy got rocked>

rolled up \ vb: [1]arrested: [2]to arrive [1]<the jail bird got __ again>

rollie \ n: a watch <nice __>

rolling deep \ vb: [1]traveling with a lot of people: [2]mobb deep [1]<his crew was __>

rollings \ n: rolling paper <his friend gave him some __>

roll out \ vb: [1]to leave: [2]dip: **-rolled out** [1]<he rolled out before the cops arrived>

rouch \ 'rōch \ n: or **roach**: a small weed cigarette, the tail end of a blunt or joint <they smoke the last of the __>

run \ vb: or **on the run** or **run da town**: [1]mandatory event: [2]referring to doing errands: [3]fleeing from the law [3]<they went on a run together>: [4]to take control or have control over things [4]<Politicians__ the town.>

run down\ vb: or **ran down**: [1]raided by the police: [2]to rob someone: *adj:* [3]fallen into partial ruin or decay [1]<The police ran down on the drug dealer> [2]<The robber was about to run down on a random person.> [3]<The house was ran down.>

run game \ vb: or **running game**: [1]to trick someone: [2]to lie to someone: [3]criminal way of thinking [1]<the girl was running game on her boyfriend>

runnin wit \ vb: [1]to ride: [2]a partnership in a particular event [1]<BJ was __ a large crew>

sag \ vb: or **sagged** or **sagging**: the wearing of pants below the waist
<the thug got a fine for sagging his pants>

salty \ 'sȯltē \ vb: feeling embarrassed by one's own mistake or by
getting proved wrong or rejected <the kid felt __ when he tripped
and fell>

say no more \ vb: [1]to affirm: [2]ok: [3]all right: [4]I hear you: [5]understood
[1]<you understand? __>

sauce\adj: or **saucy**: [1]swagger: [2]juice: [3]confident: [4]high or drunk [1]<I
got da sauce>

scadadle \ 'skå-dä-dle \ vb: to tell one to leave or to leave in general:
-scadadled <I'm about to __>

score \ vb: or **scored**: [1]to have sex with someone: [2]success in
obtaining something [2]<Mike scored with his date last night>

scrap \ 'skrap \ vb: or **scrapped** or **scrapping**: [1]to fight: [2]rumble:
[1]<they scrapped for five minutes>

screen shot \ n: a picture taken of a screen *(ex. computer screen,
phone screen, or TV screen)*

scrub \ 'skrəb \ n: [1]an inferior person: [2]a beggar or a person that
borrows but doesn't own: [3]bugaboo [2]<the __ always borrows his
friend's car>

secure \ vb: **secured** or **securing the bag** also **securing (··) bag** or
bag secured: [1]making sure one's finances are secured; [2]financial
freedom: [3]making sure money is coming in faster than it goes out
[1]<Tim worked hard to secure the bag>

selfie \ 'selfē \ n: a picture taken of one's own self using one's own
camera <she took a __ of her and her friend>

¹sellout \ n: ¹one who takes bribes or money to betray a close friend or relative: ²a traitor

²sellout \ vb: to betray for money

serial finisher\n: a person who finishes every project they start

serial starter\n: a person who starts many projects but never finishes them

set \ n: ¹a subdivision or branch of a gang: ²gang ¹<his __ controls the city

settling the score \ vb: or **settle the score** or **settled their score**: ¹to come to an agreement: ²pay back: ³truce: ³<the friends settled the score with each other>

set tripping \ vb: to disrespect a member of one's own gang or set <J was __ when he found out a member of his gang was a snitch>

seven thirty \ adj: a crazy person

sexted in \ seks-təd_ \ adv: referring to a female being initiated in a gang by having sex with the members <the girl got __ the gang>

sexting \ 'seks-tiŋ \ vb: to send nude pictures or sexual text to a person <Jake was __ his new date>

shades \ n: sunglasses <wore __ in the sun>

sharking \ 'shär-iŋ \ vb: to follow or trail a person or a thing <the undercover cop was __ the suspect>

shat \ 'shat \ adj: or **shat out**: crazy <that guy is __ for going to work naked>

shat out \ 'shat _ \ adj: ¹crazy: ²shat <you __>

sherm stick \ 'shərm_ \ n: cigarette dipped in PCP <got high off the __>

shiesty \ 'shī-ē-stē \ adj: [1]grimmy: [2]mean: [3]shady <the __ female>

shit \ n: [1]referring to anything physical or abstract: [2]jawn [1]<that __ crazy>

shited on em \ vb: to cause embarrassment or to disrespect <he __ when he pulled up in his new BMW and laughed at his haters>

shit faced \ vb: [1]wasted: [2]high: [3]drunk [1]<he was __ last night>

shorty \ 'shȯ-tē \ n: referring to one's girlfriend or a friend <your __ is pretty>

shot caller \ 'shät- \ n: [1]a boss: [2]leader of a gang [1]<women love __s>

shout out \ 'shau̇t_ \ vb: [1]to express gratitude to someone: [2]to give praise to someone [1]<__ someone on T.V.>

sick \ adj: [1]talented: [2]awesome: [3]cool: [4]good: [5]amazing: [6]on fleek: [7]hot [7]<my BMW is __>

side burns \ n: hair on the side of one's face

side chick \ n: [1]a woman other than a wife or girlfriend in which a man has a secret sexual relationship with: [2]side piece [1]<Rick has a wife and a __>

side piece \ n: side chick <he cheated on his wife with his __>

sike \ sīk \ vb: or **sike na**: [1]to take back or withdraw a prank: (*phrase*) [2]I'm just playing or I'm kidding: [3]to trick [1]<the earth stopped spinning. __>

skate \ 'skāt \ vb: to leave: **-skated** <I'm about to __>: [2]slide

skeet \ 'skēt \ vb: or **skeet skeet**: [1]to eject a fluid as sperm or semen: [2]to cum: [3]to nut: [4] to buss a nut: **-skeeted** [1]<he skeeted during sex>

skin\vb: [1]sexual intercourse: [2]a hand shake [1]<Got some _ from his wife.> [2]<His friend said, "let me get some _," then they shook hands.>

sky diver \ n: [1]a prostitute or whore: [2]a trick: [3]slut [1]<she's a __>

slammer \ 'slam-ər \ n: [1]referring to jail: [2]referring to a penis [1]<He spent five years in the __> [2]<He showed his girl his __>

slamming \ adj: [1]something delicious *(ex. food)*: [2]something appealing *(ex. a nice car or a beautiful woman)*: [3]a bad smelling odor [1]<that steak was __> [2]<she is __ hot>

slang \ 'slaŋ \ n: [1]vocabulary words randomly changed or invented to talk in codes or to brag or impress: [2]lango

slappin \ 'slap-iŋ \ adj: [1]a bad smelling odor: [2]slamming [1]<the bathroom was __ after he took a dump>

slice \ 'slīs \ vb: or **sliced**: to cut someone with a sharp object <the man got sliced up>

slide \ 'slīd \ vb: [1]to leave: [2]skate [1]<I'm about to __>

slinging \ 'sliŋ_ \ vb: [1]to sell drugs: [2]trapin [1]<the dealer was __ dope>

slipping \ 'slip-iŋ \ vb: [1]to fall off: [2]not focused: [3]failing: [4]losing: [5]caught off guard [2]<the guy was __ so he got robbed>

slow \ 'slō \ adj: a person that procrastinates or that is delusional: [2]fool: [3]dumb <you __>

sloppy seconds \ 'slä-pē \ n: something that was already used, usually referring to an ex-girlfriend or boyfriend

smash \ 'smash \ vb: or **smashed**: ¹to have sex: ²hit: ³bang ¹<he __ ed the girl>

S·M·H *(acronym)* shaking my head

S·M·M *(acronym)* Sex Money Murder gang

smoker \ n: ¹fien: ²a person that is addicted to alcohol or drugs

smut \ n: a woman of lost morals, usually sexually

¹snap \ vb: or **snapped** or **snapping**: to lash out in anger or frustration <the kid snapped on his mom>

²snaps \ n: a regular customer who buys drugs <he has a lot of __ who buy from him>

snatched up \ vb: ¹to kidnap: ²to take by force 1<the boss got __ last night>

snitch \ 'snich \ n: ¹a person that lets out secret information for personal gains or for freedom: ²rat: ³informant: ⁴stool pigeon <Gizz is a __>

snitching \ vb: ¹cooperating with the police to not get charged with a crime or cooperating to get less time in prison: ²the act of leaking information for personal favors: ³ratting: ⁴telling ¹<He was __ on his crew>

snow bunny \ n: white female

snuf \ 'snəf \ vb: or **snuffed**: to attack someone or punch in the face surprisingly

son \ n: referring to a person as cuz, mo, bro, B, etc. <what's up __>

sosa \ 'sō-sä \ n: ¹coke: ²powder ¹<he was addicted to __>

soulja hating\vb: bad mouthing a person so one can hook up with that person's spouse <Rick was soulja hating on his friend, so he could sleep with his friend's wife one day.>

soup kitchen \ vb: a sex orgy in a vehicle <they had a __ in the van>

spank \ 'spaŋk \ vb: to win in something, usually a case: **-sparked** <Tim spanked his case>

special k \ n: the street drug ketamine

speedball \ vb: to hurry or rush something or someone: **-speed balled** <he speed balled to work>

spent \ 'spent \ vb: tired <after a long day of work, she was __>

spin \ 'spin \ vb: or **spinned**: [1]to deceive: [2]to trick: [3]to beat around the bush: [4]to avoid [1]<he spinned his co-worker on the deal>

spint \ vb: to go back or to circle around <he __ around the block>

spitt-in game \ 'spit-in- \ vb: [1]to mack: [2]to rap to: [3]suductive or persuasive talk: [4]to educate someone on a particular subject [1]<he was __ to his new girl>

splif \ 'splif \ n: [1]joint: [2]blunt: [3]weed rolled up and ready to smoke [1]<the Rasta smoked a __>

[1]**spot** \ n: [1]a house: [2]a crib: [3]a dwelling place [1]<bought a new __ for his family>

[2]**spot** \ vb: or **spotted** or **spotting**: [1]to loan something: [2]to front: [3]to help someone [1]<he spotted his friend some money>

spreading (··) blows \ vb: or **spreading their blows** or **spreading your blows** or **spreading his\her blows**: to reach out to others for help <everybody got to __ from time to time>

sqoils \ 'skŏilz \ n: [1]referring to good quality of coke: [2]referring to a female's good vagina

square \ 'skwer \ n: [1]a shy or awkward person: [2]lame: [3]corny [1]<Mike is a __>

squared up \ adv: [1]two people in fighting position getting ready to fight: [2]sized up [1]<they __ before they fought>

squashing (··) beef \ 'skwäsh-iŋ_ \ n: a truce between two parties who were at odds: squashed (··) beef *(interject the proper adjective his, her, my or their)* <squashing his beef>

stacks \ 'stakz \ n: a thousand dollars or referring to a lot of money <the rapper brought a lot of __ to the club>

stash \ 'stash \ n: [1]referring to money hidden *(ex. in a bank or in a safe)*: [2]a hidden location [1]<hid a million in his __>

statistic \ 'stə-'tis-tik \ adj: [1]a victim of cheating: [2]a victim of violence or incarceration [1]<my sister just made the __>

stay fly \ 'stā_ \ vb: or **staying fly**: [1]phrase used to compliment an already fly person: [2]keep up the good work [1]<__ bro!>

[1]**steel** \'stēl \ vb: or **stoled**: to punch <he was getting ready to steel Jeff>

[2]**steel** \ n: referring to a gun <a concealed __ in his waist>

stepped on \ 'step-əd _ \ vb: to stretch cocaine with baking soda to make more crack <that coke is __>

stick up kid \ n: robber

stoned \ 'stōn-əd \ vb: high on drugs usually referring to being high on weed <they got __>

stool pigeon \ 'stül-'pi-jəl \ n: ¹a snitch: ²rat: ³informant ¹<the __ still went to jail after his testimony>

straight \ 'strāt \ adj: ¹OK: ²I'm fine ¹<I'm __>

¹strap \ 'strap \ n: a gun <he had a __>

²strap \ adj: being armed <he was __> strapped

strap up\adv: or **strapped up**: using protection during sex

streets \ 'strēt \ n: or **streets**: ¹referring to anywhere outside of jail or police custody: ²local neighborhood in a town or city: *(phrase)* ³**In the** __: lifestyle of alleged criminal activities: ⁴__**knowledge**: common sense learned on or about the street *(see definition 2)*

street code \ n: the moral standards of how to operate in the streets *(ex. never snitch, never rape or molest children, no homosexuality, never befriend a snitch, homosexual, or rapist, and always get money) *some cities very and have different codes*

street creds \ n: ¹popularity: ²cool points: ³one's credibility status according to the streets or industry ³<most rappers lose their __ after getting famous>

street dude \ n: ¹someone with the knowledge of the pros and cons of the street: ²someone that hustles in the community and gives back: ³a person from the street ¹<the intelligent __>

street level \ n: status quo in the street <he improved his__>

street sweeper \ n: a high capacity rifle *(ex. AK-47 or Tommy gun)* <he used a __ to flee from the police>

stunt in \ 'stənt-in \ vb: ¹the showing off one's own riches: ²bragging about one's own wealth: ³balling: ⁴flashy <people with a lot of money love to stunt>

style \ n: [1]swagger: [2]fashionable [1]<I like her __>

sucka \ 'sək-kä \ n: [1]loser: [2]busta: [3]square: [4]one in the way of progress [1]<some people are real __s>

sucka free \ vb: [1]not around a sucka: [2]conflict free: [3]clear from lames: *(phrase)* [4]I'm good [1]<I stay __>

suga \ 'shủ-gä \ n: a kiss <I gave my grandmother some __ when I saw her>

sugar daddy \ n: a man that sponsors a female <her __ has a lot of money>

sugar mommy \ n: a female that sponsors a male <his __ pays all the bills>

superbad \ adj: [1]referring to a very attractive female: [2]badd: [3]dime: [1]<my girlfriend is __>

swag \ 'swag \ n: a person's unique style <he got __>

swagger \ 'swa-gər \ n: [1]fashionable sense: [2]the way a person dresses [1]<most famous people have __>

swaggeriffic \ 'swag-gər-ē-fik \ adj: [1]plenty of swagger: [2]perfect swagger: [3]thorouel: [4]feeling overly confident [1]<Tom felt __ after he bought a Benz>

swagger jackier \ n: a person that copy cats a person style <my brother is such a __>

swagger jacking \ vb: to steal a person's style <he was __ his friend>

sweet \ 'swēt \ adj: [1]easy: [2]soft: [3]cowardly: [4]scared [1]<that dude is __>

sweting \ 'swet-in \ vb: or **swet**: [1]to pursue a person or a situation without patience non-stop: [2]on his top [1]<stop __ me>

tag him

.

the boysT

tag him \ 'tag_ \ vb: or **tagged him**: to shoot someone <I'm about to __>

tanked\ 'tanked\vb: [1]drunk: [2]wasted

tap out \ 'tap_ \ vb: or **tapped out** or **tapping out**: [1]to give up or surrender: [2]to cop out [1]<tapped out of the fight>

taking the cake \ vb: or **took the cake**: to win a prize <When I won, I took the cake>

taking the rap \ vb: or **took the rap** or **take the rap**: to take the blame for a crime someone else did <took the rap for his friend>

talking fly\vb: or **popping fly**: [1]trash talk: [2]to exaggerate

talk in turkey \ vb: getting down to business <let's __>

T·C·B *(acronym)* take care of business

teener \ 'tēn-ər \ n: a half of an 8 ball

telling \ 'tel-in \ vb: [1]snitching: [2]ratting: [3]told [1]<his cousin was __ on him in court.>

telly \ 'telē \ n: [1]a hotel: [2]a phone [1]<Pete took his side chick to the __>

tender dick \adj: or **tender dicking**: [1]a male that is sensitive or over protective with females: [2]a man who lets women take advantage of him [1]<My friend is _ when it comes to women>

the boys \ n: [1]the police: [2]po-po: [3]five-o: [4]thugs [1]<__ surrounded the block>

the third wheel \ adj: the third person tagging along on a date between two people

thorouel \ 'ther-ō \ n: [1]ill: [2]real: [3]authentic: [4]a person, place or thing without a flaw [4]<the __ car>

thorouel bread \ n: [1]a person that mastered his/her characters: [2]real: [3]ill

thot \ 'thät \ n: [1]a whore: [2]that hoe over there: [3]thristy

thirsty \ adj: [1]a desperate or a broke person: [2]dirty

throw or **threw** or **thrown** or **throwing (··) under the bus** \ vb: to place blame on someone

throw down \ adv: being good at something *(ex. good cook or good in bed)* <my dad knows how to __ in the kitchen>

throwing shade \ vb: [1]to start controversy: [2]beef [1]<Dan was __ at Jess>

thug \ n: a ruthless fearless person without morals

thump \ vb: or **thumping**: [1]to fight: [2]brawl [3]shake: [4]tip

thunder breed \ n: an ambitious new member in a gang *(see breeds)*

tick \ n: [1]jail time: [2]time in general [1]<his brother was doing some in jail>

tick off \ vb: or **ticked off**: [1]to get angry: [2]to flip: [3]tight [1]<the ticked off man >

[1]tight \ adj: [1]something that is beautiful or appealing to the eye: [2]on fleek: [3]hot: [4]popin [1]<that house was __>

[2]tight \ vb: [1]to get mad or upset: [2]to be stingy with something [1]<my dad was __ after he lost the house>

time piece \ n: ¹a watch: ²a rollie ¹<the expensive __>

tip \ vb: ¹to fight: ²tick-off: ³tight: ⁴ angry: ⁵to give information: - **tipped** ¹<tipped on his friend> ⁵<tipped the cops with information>

tip drill \ 'tip_ \ n: referring to a female's booty, usually a stripper <she got a __>

tipping \ 'tip-iŋ \ vb: see outta pocket

tipsy \ 'tip-sē \ vb: buzzed from alcohol <the __ driver>

toke \ 'tōk \ vb: ¹possession of a gun: ²strapped ¹<to __ a gun> - **toking**

token \ 'tō-kən \ n: ¹a black person being used or trying to fit in with the whites: ²uncle tom

top \ vb: ¹referring to a person receiving oral sex: ²head: ³brains: - **topped** ¹<the girl gave him __>

top six \ n: Haitian gang

track \ 'trā-k \ n: a song

track record \ n: ¹a person's history usually not a criminal record, but more so a social record *(ex. sex history)* ¹<she had a clean __ with boys>: ²reputation

train reck \ 'trān-'rek \ adj: ugly or messy <that girl is a __>

trap \ 'trap \ n: ¹a place where people buy drugs: ² the game: ³the hood ¹<selling drugs in the __>

trappin \ vb: ¹selling drugs: ²drug distribution ¹<__ to get money>

trashed \ vb: ¹a person getting beat up: ²to lose a fight ¹<that kid got __ by the cop>

trash talk \ vb: to instigate or provoke with words: **-trash talking** <trash talking led to the fight>

treated \ 'trēt \ vb: [1]trashed: [2]beaten up: [3]to lose a fight [2]<the guy got __ so bad that he had to go to the hospital>

tree \ 'trē \ n: weed <smoked __>

trendsetter \ n: [1]a person that set trends or creates a fad: [2]one who sets a standard [1]<the confident __>

trending \ 'trend-in \ vb: a hot topic being talked about on social media <I wonder what's __ online>

trick \ 'trik \ n: [1]a prostitute: [2]smut: [3]hooker: [4]freak [1]<that __ gave me an STD>

tricking \ vb: to spend money for pleasure *(ex. a man spending money on a female to sleep with her)* <the guy was __ on his new girlfriend>

trifling \ 'trī-flin \ adj: dirty or nasty <the __ rug>

triple nine \ adj: code name used to identify a snitch *(see bloods)*

triple og \ n: [1]gangsta: [2]an og: [3]a boss

trippin \ 'trip- pē \ vb: [1]to fuss and argue: [2]crazy

trippy \ 'trip-pē \ vb: [1]getting high: [2]wasted: [3]litt [1]<they got __>

true \ adv: [1]correct: [2]yes

trumming \ 'trŭm-in \ vb: [1]customers and clients consistently coming in: [2]success in business [1]<the store was __>

tryin ah play me \ vb: phrase used when someone is trying to trick, lie, or deceive a person <why you __?>

T·T·Y·L *(acronym)* talk to you later

tube \ n: a TV

tune in \ vb: to give attention to: **-tuned in** <__ to the T.V.>

tune out \ vb: to ignore or to take attention from: **-tuned out** <__ the T.V.>

turbo \ n: [1]weed mixed with cocaine: [2]angel dust [1]<got high off __>

turf \ 'tərf \ n: one's territory <one's __>

turkey \ n: [1]a female's butt, booty, etc.: [2]ass: [3]cake [1]<she got a big __>

turn down \ vb: or **turned down**: [1]a state of displeasure or normality: [2]low: [3]boring: [4]uncomfortable: [5]sad: [6]rejected [3]<this party is __>

turn up \ vb: or **turn it up** or **turned up**: [1]a state of excitement: [2]joy: [3]confidence: [4]pleasure: [5]to fight: [6]amped up: [7]enjoyment [2]<this party is __>

twat \ n: [1]a vagina: [2]box

twat blocking \ vb: [1]to interfere or stop a female from having sex: [2]cock blocking [1]<Jessica was __ her friend>

[1]**tweek** \ vb: to adjust something *(ex. a screw)*: **-tweeked** <tweeked the sound of the music>

[2]**tweek** \ n: [1]a trick: [2]ho: [3]smut: [4]freak: [5]bitch [1]<the money hungry __>

twerk \ vb: a dance move involving shaking or giggling the butt

twerly \ vb: [1]to receive oral sex: [2]head: [3]top [1]<the guy got a __ from his girl>

twist \ n: [1]a hobby: [2]whatever someone likes to do [1]<what is your __>

twista \ n: [1]a gun: [2]a strap: [3]nina [1]<was armed with a __>

twisted \ vb: [1]to be misunderstood: [2]high or drunk: [3]to be under estimated [3]<that guy got me __>

twisting \ vb: [1]fighting: [2]referring to killing someone [1]<they were __> [2]<he was __ him>

type time *(phrase)* [1]what are you up to?: [2]what is he up to?: *(ex. when someone is doing something out of order)* <what __ he on?>

2·on \ 'tü- \ vb: or **two-on**: drunk and high at the same time <she was __>

ugh \ adv: [1]used in text, to express agitation: [2]saddness: [3]tiredness

Uncle Sam \ n: [1]to US treasury: [2]the government

Uncle Tom \ n: a person that loves another race more than his or her own *(ex. usually an African American loving the white race more than his own)*

under dog \ n: [1]a person least expected to win: [2]an underrated person

up \ adj: [1]having a lot of money: [2]being successful at a task [1]<Ray is __>

up the river \ vb: referring to someone going to prison

u wee \ n: U-turn

vee \ n: [1]a car: [2]a whip: [3]a ride [1]<he took a ride in his __>

viral \ 'vi-rəl \ vb: [1]something being talked about by everyone usually online *(ex. a video or a picture or a comment)* [1]<the video went __ in one hour>: [2]trending

violation \ ˌvī-ə-lā-shən \ vb: [1]to disrespect: [2]punishment: [3]to violate

wack \ 'wak \ adv: [1]corny: [2]boring or unentertaining [1]<that song was __>

wagon \ 'wa-gən \ n: [1]referring to a female's phat ass: [2]donkey: [3]badunkadunk: [4]ass [1]<she got a nice __>

wake and bake *(phrase)* wake up and get high off weed or other drugs

wakeup \ n or adj: a hit of drugs or referring to drugs or coffee

wamming \ 'wäm-in \ adj: something good *(ex. good food)* <that chicken was __>

wansta \ 'wän-sta \ n: a fake gangsta <the new rapper is a __>

wasted \ 'wāst-ed \ vb: to be drunk or high <the girl got __>

wat it do *(phrase)* what's up or what's going on, usually used in the southern states

wat it hittin fo *(phrase)* [1]what's up: [2]wat it do: [3]wat's popin: [4]wat's da structure [1]<__bro?>

wats da structure *(phrase)* [1]what's going on or what's the plan: [2]wat it do: [3]wat's popin [1]<__ bro?>

wats popin *(phrase)* [1]what's up: [2]wat it hittin fo: [3]wat it do: [4]wats da structure [1]<__bro?>

wavy \ 'wā-vē \ vb: [1]feeling good or fly: [2]high: [3]litt [1]<after smoking some weed, the girl was feeling __>

waxing dat \ 'waks-in-dat \ vb: [1]smashing: [2]to hit: [3]aggresive sex: wax dat [1]<she wanted him to wax dat>

weed \ 'wēd n: [1]marijuana: [2]tree: [3]green: [4]marley

¹weight \ 'wāt \ n: referring to drugs *(ex. pounds of weed or kilos of cocaine)* <the drug dealer sells __>

²weight \ vb: or **holding weight** or **packing weight**: ¹token: ²to have a gun: ³strapped ²<Tim was packing weight>

weinne \ 'wē·nē \ n: ¹a lame person: ²a drug addict or fien ²<Jessica is a __>

went postal \ vb: or **going postal**: to go on a killing rampage or lose one's temper

wet \ 'wet \ n: ¹P.C.P.: ²weed dipped in embalming fluid: ³wiggles: ⁴referring to a horny female ¹<got high off __>

wet back\n: derogatory term used to degrade a Hispanic person

wet up \ vb: ¹to make someone bleed by way of shooting with a gun: ²to get shot ¹<Gary got __ last night>

¹whip \ 'hwip \ n: ¹a car ¹<the fast __> adj: ²one being controlled by their spouse, usually emotionally

²whip \ vb: to turn powder cocaine into crack: **-whipped** <whipped up some coke>

³whip \ vb: knowing how to do something really well *(ex. cooking or driving a car)* <Dad can sure __ up some food?

whipped \ 'hwip-ped \ vb: ¹being infatuated with a person: ²letting someone get their way despite their own wishes because of an emotional attachment: ³sprung ¹<my sister is so __ by her boyfriend>

whipper snapper \ n: a baby or a young person

white girl \ n: ¹cocaine: ²Justin Bieber ¹<the drug dealer sells __>

white wash \ adj: [1]formal English: [2]writing that is formal [1]<the urban author thought that a popular publisher was trying to __ his manuscript>

wicked\ 'wi-kƏd\adj: *(Jamaican Slang)*: [1]to compliment excellence in a thing *(ex. a song)*: *syn* [2]on fleek: [3]hot: [4]fire [1]<That song is a _ song.>

wify \ 'wīf·ē \ n: a girlfriend that acts as if she is a wife <you my __>

wig \ 'wig \ n: [1]the head: [2]the upper part of the body containing the brain: [3]nagon [1]<put a hat on his __>

wigger \ 'wig-ger \ n: [1]a white person who is not from the hood but tries to act like it: *(contraction)* [2]wanna be nigger

wiggles \ 'wi-gles \ n: [1]wet: [2]PCP [2]<to smoke __>

wildin out \ vb: [1]crunk: [2]acting crazy: [3]having fun [3]<they were __ at the club>

window shopper \ n: a person who can't afford to buy goods, so they just look at things they like <the broke __>

window shopping \ vb: to browse and not buy <the rapper was __>

wip \ 'wip \ vb: or **wipped**: [1]to beat up someone: [2]being beaten up [1]<I'm about to __ your ass>

wit dat \ n: [1]the approval of: [2]the accepting of: [3]the accompany of, are you down? [1]<I'm __>

wiz \ 'wīz \ vb: [1]to be high: [2]litt: [3]wavy: [4]on one [1]<my friend was __ high last night>

wolfing \ 'wůlf-iŋ \ adj :[1]hairy: *vb:* [2]to eat food in a rush [1]<I was __ so I had to get a haircut> [2]<_ down the food.>

wolf packing\vb: [1]mulitple guys having sex with a female one after the other: [2]train

word \ 'wərd \ adv: [1]really: [2]in agreement to something: [3]to question something: [4]to agree with (ex. OK): [5]solid [1]<I love my mother. __!> [3]<I won the lotto. __?>

word to mother \ vb: [1]to swear: [2]to exaggerate a point: [3]truth [1]<__, I had sex with her> [2]<I'm so rich, __>

word up \ adv: to agree with <I love my family. __>

work \ n: [1]drugs: [2]a pack <the dealer had a lot of __>

wu tang \ 'wǔ-tan \ n: the name of a dance <the boy was doing the __>

X

.

x \ 'eks \ n: ecstasy

x'ed out \ vb: [1]murdered: [2]bodied: [3]to get rid of a plan

yall \ n: you all

ya mean *(phrase)* you know what I mean

yams \ n: [1]a vagina: [2]twat: [3]box

yankee \ n: an American

yardie \ n: a Jamaican

yellow bone \ n: a light skinned African American woman

yo blood \ 'yō_ \ *(interjection)* used to call attention or indicate attentiveness or express affirmation

you ain't bout dat life \ adv: a phrase used when telling someone that they are not fit for a particular life style

you smoking *(phrase)* you crazy

youngan \ 'yən-gan \ n: [1]young man or young blood: [2]young buck [1]<what's up __?>

young blood \ n: [1]youngan: [2]young buck [1]<come here __>

young buck \ n: a person under the age of 25 years, usually used by elders to address a young person <__, get me some water>

yow \ interj: [1]hey: [2]yo blood: [3]used to call attention to

yu aint bout dat (phrase) [1]you liar: [2]you a fraud: [3]you ain't about that life

yu already know (phrase) [1]to agree with: [2]word: [3]yes [1]<you coming right?>

yu dig \ vb: [1]understand: [2]dig me [1]<I got a master plan, __?>

yu doin it \ n: a compliment to someone that is successful

yu keepin up wit da Jones *(phrase)* are you keeping up with the latest trends

zanies

.

zzz's

zanies \ 'zā-nēs \ n: a downer drug in pill form

zap \ 'zap \ vb: or **zapped**: to be high, usually from zanies

zoe \ 'zō \ n: a Haitian person

zoe pound \ n: a Haitian gang

zooted \ 'züt-ed \ vb: [1]high on drugs: [2]wavy: [3]litt: [4]wiz

zzz's \ zē \ adj: sleep